Myra Hess

Photo: Daniel Farson

MYRA HESS
(1890–1965)

Myra Hess

BY HER FRIENDS

COMPILED BY

DENISE LASSIMONNE

EDITED AND WITH AN INTRODUCTION BY

HOWARD FERGUSON

Illustrated

HAMISH HAMILTON
LONDON

First published in Great Britain, 1966
by Hamish Hamilton Ltd
90 Great Russell Street London WC1

Copyright © Hamish Hamilton, 1966
Discography © F. F. Clough and G. J. Cuming, 1966

Printed in Great Britain by
Western Printing Services Ltd, Bristol

Contents

v

Contents

Illustrations

Preface

THIS MEMORIAL volume is in no sense a biography of Dame Myra Hess, nor does it attempt to provide a full account of her career. It is, rather, a collection of informal sketches by some of her friends, each of whom concentrates on a somewhat different aspect of her life or personality. No attempt has been made to edit away an occasional inconsistency or duplication of material, as the slightly differing viewpoints of the writers help to produce a likeness that is more rounded and at the same time not unfaithful.

Some parts of Myra's life are less fully covered than others. It is rarely remembered, for example, that her climb to fame was so far from sudden that for many years she had to support herself by teaching. Early records kept by her mother show, too, that her repertoire then included works that were later dropped, and that the fees she received were small. At her début at Queen's Hall on 14 November 1907, when the conductor was young Mr. Thomas Beecham, she played not only the Beethoven G major Concerto, as one might expect, but also the Saint-Saëns in C minor; and, even more surprisingly, rounded off the programme with a couple of solos by Chopin. At her first Promenade Concert on 2 September 1908 she played the Liszt E flat Concerto for the magnificent fee of three guineas. And in November of the same year, at a recital in Bournemouth shared with Szigeti, her part of the programme consisted of the Brahms E flat *Rhapsody*, the Franck *Prelude, Chorale and Fugue*, and two pieces by Liszt, for which her fee of £4 5s. yielded a net profit of £1 15s. after expenses had been paid.

Few people know, too, that in later life an enormous amount of her time was devoted to things quite unconnected with her own career. At the period of the National Gallery Concerts she coined a catch-phrase, 'Sign please', to indicate that some official had been either wheedled or bludgeoned into a course of action that was essential for the welfare of the Concerts. From that time on, however, it was she herself who was often invited to 'sign please' on behalf of some cause that would benefit by her fame and the liveliness of her interest. She served on committees of the wartime Council for the Encouragement of Music and the Arts, and of the later Arts Council, the British Council, and the Federation of Business and Professional Women; she was a member of the Treasury Advisory Committee that reported on grants for schools of music, and of the Council of her own beloved Royal Academy of Music; and she was of vital help to the British Institute of Recorded Sound at a critical juncture of its evolution. Indeed, she lived such a full life, and so many people grew to depend on her, that it is hardly surprising if certain aspects of it find no mention in the following pages.

The idea of the book was Denise Lassimonne's, and she it was who approached most of the contributors. She then handed over the editing to me, with the result that I was able to persuade her that she herself should write the section on Myra and Tobias Matthay, her old teacher.

Both Miss Lassimonne and I would like to express our warmest thanks to all those who have made the book possible: to the contributors, who not only agreed to write their essays in the middle of busy lives but actually produced them by the date required; to the various photographers whose pictures add such a welcome dimension to this informal portrait; to Professor W. K. C. Guthrie for allowing his speech at the Cambridge honorary degree ceremony to be reprinted; to Mr. F. F. Clough and Dr. G. J. Cuming for their Discography, originally compiled for *Recorded Sound*, the journal of the British Institute of Recorded Sound; and to its editor, Mr. Patrick Saul, for allowing it to be included here. Miss Beryl Davis, Myra's niece, and Miss Anita Gunn, her secretary, have given constant help and encouragement, and have supplied invaluable information at every turn.

Preface

All the contributors have generously agreed that the pro-
ceeds of the book should be given to the Myra Hess Trust.
This fund has been established as a memorial to Myra and
her work, and its aim is to help professional musicians in a
variety of ways, all of which would have been close to her
heart. Anyone who wishes to join in this tribute should send
their donation to: The Secretary, The Myra Hess Trust,
c/o F. J. Ronald–Eric White Associates Ltd., Melbourne
House, Aldwych, London, W.C.2.

HOWARD FERGUSON

Remembering Dame Myra Hess

BY

JOHN MASEFIELD

Glad memories come, of old, long-distant days
When I, with many hundreds, saw and heard,
And joined with many hundreds in her praise,
Glad memories, all, with no remembered word,
But with the sense that she who played perceived
The world undying, that composers know
At moments, as reward for years of woe,
She touched that deathless world and we believed.

Death to such souls is as a night in May
When a small bird's ecstatic throat declares
Beauty undying to the moonlit airs
Blending both Death and Night in deathless day.

A Unique Friendship

BY

IRENE SCHARRER

M Y FRIENDSHIP with Myra from early childhood to within a few days of her passing was a very wonderful, very rare experience. We became devoted to one another in childhood—before that our mothers had been friends.

I first remember Myra coming to the Royal Academy for her lesson with Uncle Tobs when she was twelve years old. She brought some silly little piece by Eduard Schütt and I must confess to being a little shocked! That soon changed: she inspired in me real affection and admiration, and we became inseparable friends. At that time she looked rather like the photograph facing page 4, but with her hair drawn back more tightly from her forehead. This was quite unbearable to me, and so unlike her dear little personality. A fellow-student and I removed the ribbon and freed her lovely hair, deciding that her appearance must be taken in hand.

A few years later she took me in hand! On one occasion, when I was playing two concertos at the Albert Hall, she came to the artists' room in the interval in a state of horror to tell me that I had put my dress on back-to-front. She literally tore it off me, and then sent me on to the platform looking considerably more presentable. This is only a tiny example of her insistence on my looking and playing my best. It was part of her nature to care desperately for one's well being. I always felt that whatever made for joy or sorrow in my life affected her in a very special way.

After our lessons in the old R.A.M. building in Tenterden Street, we used to walk together to Oxford Circus, where I could pick up my bus for home. But by the time we got there we were so engrossed in our conversation that I would insist on turning back and walking to Myra's bus-stop at the foot of Baker Street, half a mile away in the opposite direction, very often three or four times before we could bring ourselves to part.

My visits to her home were full of fun and laughter, and I can remember her mother finding us giggling helplessly one bedtime, when we should have been fast asleep, and tucking us up with a mild protest and a rhyme that was then current: 'You naughty kittens, You've lost your mittens!' Nor were these the only times when we were overcome by giggles. At one time poor Mr. Corder, our long-suffering harmony professor, took us by the shoulders and put us out of his room when he found our nonsense unendurable. And years later, Arnold Bax in his autobiography was to look back on us as 'two giggling schoolgirls'.

Whilst still Academy students we began giving two-piano recitals together—or, as John Galsworthy's sister used to call them, 'My-rene recitals'. They were always the greatest joy. We appeared in London and the provinces and in America, playing everything from the Mozart Sonata to the Saint-Saens Variations on a theme by Beethoven, with the Arensky Waltz as a never-failing encore. Arnold Bax wrote for us his tone-poem 'Moy Mell', and this too we loved to include in our programmes.

We always addressed one another as 'B.G.', a name that arose in a ridiculous way. One day when I was practising in my home at Eton, and Myra was staying with me, she came into my studio, swept me a curtsey and exclaimed, 'Goddess!' Not to be outdone, and thinking of a famous pair of cross-talk comedians, The Brothers So-and-so, I made her an even deeper curtsey and replied, 'Brother Goddess!' So 'B.G.' we remained to each other for all time.

Hers was the most brilliant wit I have ever known, with an almost infectious delight in nonsense. She would sing that terrible song 'The Rosary' in a rich, plummy contralto voice, a semitone flat throughout—that in itself was really a brilliant achievement, as anyone would know who tried to do it. And then her singing of 'The Jewel Song' from Gounod's *Faust*, while I tinkled out her accompaniment on the piano, was never to be forgotten. On one such occasion Landon Ronald was present; and to my disappointment and surprise he seemed quite unable even to smile, though the rest of the party was rocking with laughter. When asked if he were not amused, to my amazement he said perfectly seriously, 'Not at all, I was *much* too moved by the sheer beauty of her voice and the artistry of her singing.' At one of our two-piano concerts—I think it was in Birmingham— we were both suffering from a bad attack of flu. As we walked off the platform at the end of the programme Myra remarked, 'What perfect ensemble! We even sniff and cough in unison.'

She relished, too, any absurd incident that happened to her friends, and would never allow me to forget the time in the early days of my motoring career, and in the dead of night, when I had a slight mishap with a lamp post, which was flat on the ground with my car astride. The car, if not the lamp post, appeared to be quite undamaged, so with a sigh of relief I continued on my way. But alas, a few days later a policeman arrived at our front door bearing in his hand, of all things, my number-plate. My husband remarked, 'Did you *have* to leave your visiting-card?'

Each of us could always rely on the other in any emergency. So I was never surprised during the war years when Myra would telephone a last-minute S.O.S.: 'My darling, could you possibly play with me at the Gallery today? So-and-so is ill, and I'm in despair.' Once, when the casualty happened to be a man, Myra made a little speech to the audience when we went on the platform, and I suddenly heard her thanking me for coming at such short notice, and for so kindly stepping into Mr. So-and-so's breeches. Realizing what she had said, she doubled up with laughter and the whole audience was in an uproar.

MYRA AS A CHILD

MYRA AGED 12

MYRA AGED 15

MYRA AGED 19

Photo: Elliot and Fry

Another memorable National Gallery occasion was on New Years' Day 1940, when eight or nine of us took part in Schumann's *Carnaval*, playing turn and turn about on two pianos. Later in the programme Sir Kenneth Clark made a dashing appearance as conductor of the Haydn Toy Symphony, in which Elena Gerhardt played a toy drum, Benno Moiseiwitsch a triangle, and Myra and I a pair of cuckoos. (They were temperamental birds and sometimes oo-ed before they cuck-ed.) It was a wonderful performance —but oh! how we laughed.

I seem to have stressed the lighter side of our relationship, but it was a very deep and beautiful friendship, and in the very last year we seemed to be even closer than ever before. Myra's devotion was unswerving; and in every crisis of my life her understanding and infinite wisdom helped me along the way. Her single-mindedness of purpose was in itself an inspiration. She was willing to sacrifice everything in life for her music; and her distress was genuine when it became clear that I could not rule out marriage and the desire for children, for she knew that they would inevitably come first in my life—and how right she was! And yet, there was always her desire to share in all their successes, joys and sorrows.

One incident of her deep feeling and touching sympathy stands out in my memory. At the time of my mother's passing, she telephoned to say she must be with me at the funeral. I explained that I felt I must be absolutely alone— not even my family were to be present. She was deeply distressed for me, and begged to be allowed just to sit in her car outside the grounds so that I should know she was near—unforgettable compassion and tenderness.

Though I seemed tempted to grieve over her passing, I later was able to realize that the *qualities* we all loved— her true spiritual being—could never die and must be eternal. Then I could only be thankful—and indeed I am.

Early Days

BY

CLARE MACKAIL

. . . those first affections
Those shadowy recollections
Which, be they what they may,
Are yet the fountain-light of all our day . . .
WORDSWORTH

MYRA FIRST came into our lives in 1914, when she
spent several months alone at Rottingdean in order
to work undisturbed. There she met my grandmother,[1] and on her return to London came to my parents'
home where I first met her and heard her play. The impression was immediate and profound. It seemed too good
to be true: a human being and an artist of such golden integrity, yet it was borne out over fifty years.

Among the first qualities one became aware of were sincerity and humility, together with an innocence, a guile-
lessness which in those days was almost over-credulous, and
an extraordinary faculty of sympathy which was able to
overcome a natural reserve. This sympathy was of the very
rare kind that enables one to stand in someone else's shoes
and see with their eyes, and which brings relief or encouragement less from counsel or action than from the quality of
listening and understanding, and above all of caring. This
does not mean that she was lacking in practical help; indeed
the extent and generosity of this all through her life will
never be known, but even more was this faculty of identifying herself with others, which meant that she really felt
their joys and sorrows as her own.

[1] Lady Burne-Jones, the widow of the painter Sir Edward Burne-
Jones. (Ed.)

It soon became evident that these qualities were matched by an inspired sense of humour which enchanted everyone who knew her. Although the clouds of four years of war were gathering, and although she had her measure of personal sorrows and struggles, yet some of the clearest memories of these young days are of laughter, of fun, even of gaiety. She was a unique raconteuse and mimic, and no one who heard and saw her imitations of a lodging-house piano with its dumb notes, or of a pianola playing Chopin, or of 'The Jewel Song' from *Faust*, can ever forget their brilliance.

But beneath all this one never lost the sense of deep purpose: the unremitting labour to become a more worthy servant of music and of her fellow beings.

At this time she was emerging from family misfortunes and was living in lodgings and teaching long hours, playing a good deal in public and of course practising, often far into the night. In an account book of this time is the entry in red ink of her first three-guinea fee. Her concert dresses cost mostly only a few pounds, but though very simple were often a splendid colour. She was well built and rather short, yet gave the impression on the platform of being almost tall and slender, and her appearance was very impressive, the noble and expressive brow and bearing, the swift grace of the walk on and off the platform, and the long, deep bow which was to remain so characteristic all her life.

Although she was working so hard there were occasional holidays, though nearly always where a piano was available and where she could go on practising. First among these must always come the visits to High Marley, the hill-top home of her beloved teacher, Tobias Matthay, and his wife 'Auntie Jessie', whose profound influence on her whole life is described elsewhere in these pages.[1] The place was magical, with its vast changing views, its pure air, the sound of larks, the smell of woodsmoke, the walks on the heights or in the beechwoods, the enthralling talk, the timeless meals, the laughter, the music and the hours of study. It gave Myra,

[1] See p. 17: 'Myra and Uncle Tobs', by Denise Lassimonne. (Ed.)

almost from childhood, her first real opportunity of finding her true self and of setting her compass.

Then there were the happy times spent at a cottage on Cumnor Hill near Oxford, where after a concert in the city, young and older would gather for what became a kind of impromptu festival going on for several days, and including music-making, expeditions, supper parties and again much laughter. Undergraduates, many of them in training or on leave from war service, would sit on the floor while Myra played whatever was asked for on a little upright piano, only breaking off for meals and more laughter. Sir Hugh Allen, then organist at New College, would often join in, and it was at this time that she first heard the Bach chorale, 'Jesu, Joy of Man's Desiring', which later became so associated with her in her own piano arrangement. It was in Oxford too, during some charades in which Myra also took part, that Dr. Ernest Walker, the distinguished and learned musician, gave an inspired performance as the serpent in the Garden of Eden.

Among the clearest pictures of those days is of an expedition to my grandmother at Rottingdean. A long walk over the downs, our arrival at the white house on the village green, an enfolding welcome and a meal, and then Myra playing to her, again on a little upright piano, surrounded by my grandfather's Grail-Quest pictures and the William Morris curtains and carpets; a bright fire burning in the grate and my grandmother's minute form and wondering eyes, listening as though the gates of heaven were ajar. The little room gently glowed with sound and colour. Most specially there remains the playing of some Beethoven Bagatelles and of the Brahms E flat Intermezzo, so exquisitely adjusted to the size both of my grandmother and of the room.

In those days one could still walk into a concert or a theatre not long before the curtain went up; and after this perfect day of walking, sun, air and music, Myra suggested ending up at the Diaghilev Ballet, and was rewarded by *The Good-Humoured Ladies* and *Boutique Fantasque* with

Lopokova and Massine. Her enjoyment was quite indescribable in its freshness and effervescence: she almost literally danced in her seat.

Going to a concert with her too was always a revelation. Her listening was so total, and so engaged her whole being that it was contagious and one heard many things one would otherwise have missed; to this day there are certain passages which are still heard through her ears. Yet where someone else, even as a listener, might quite unconsciously have imposed their own conception upon one, this was never so with her. Her reverence for music meant that she was always the learner, often even the beginner. Up to the end she was never satisfied with her own performances, always ready to listen to a sincere opinion, always working at the music itself, communing with it, listening to what it had to say. Much of this work was done in silence, sometimes with the music and the keyboard before her, sometimes during a meal alone, or a game of patience. It seems that this silent work was some of the most important of all, and that this same attitude was perhaps the secret of much of her genius for personal relationships where her capacity for deep listening appeared to be limitless.

A new chapter in her life opened at about this time, when she moved into the first real home of her own in Carlton Hill, St. John's Wood. There was a large studio built over part of the garden, and this was to be a great joy and blessing to her and to everyone who visited it for many years. There would be happy gatherings there after concerts, long hours of study, chamber music, lessons, friends to meals and always the open-armed welcome at the foot of the studio stairs. It seemed natural on Armistice Day that friends converged upon this room, and finding Myra rehearsing with string players, that this turned into a thanksgiving concert. In those days too some young music-lovers would often meet to sing part songs, madrigals or carols, and would sometimes end up by serenading Myra, who instead of giving us a tip to go away, invariably invited us to come in, and often

rewarded us with her own music. Among those who sometimes joined in was the young Adrian Boult, and rehearsals
would often take place on the open top of a bus en route.

The death of Myra's father brought her even closer to her
mother, whose courage, humour and devotion were abiding
influences all her life. In later years when it became clear
that her mother's last illness would be prolonged, she at
once cancelled an American tour and installed her mother
in her own bedroom, spending every possible hour with her,
caring for her, amusing her, solacing her. Her death left a
gap that could never be filled, and Myra often spoke of these
months as some of the most precious of her whole life.

Another unforgettable picture of those far off days is of a
summer holiday which she spent with us. We had hired
an upright piano for her to practise on, and she insisted on
going to meet it in the carrier's open horse-drawn cart,
already half filled with packages. When the piano was safely
loaded on she managed to climb in and seat herself on a crate
within reach of the keyboard; from this precarious position,
and on an unmetalled road, she played for nearly all of the
three miles home. When we reached the gates not only was
she already sitting askew, but as the steep descent of the
drive began, she was also tilted increasingly sideways. This
in no way deterred her, and the lovely strains of Ravel's
Pavane pour une Infante Défunte soared above the scraping
of the brakes. Neither horse nor driver appeared in the least
impressed, though this was undoubtedly one of her most
outstanding performances.

There were very happy gatherings too in our London
home when by some miracle and at very short notice many
busy people, musicians and war workers, all seemed to be
free or on leave together. One of these gatherings went on
for 48 hours with many spending the night on mattresses
on the floor so that music could begin again in the morning.
A group of young musicians even arrived from Birmingham,
among them Dorothy Silk and Anthony Bernard. String,
and even wind players sprang up from nowhere, the carpet

was rolled back, music stands put out, and we were off! Myra played the Bach D minor Concerto with strings most of whom had never met before, but whom she gathered up and fused. Campbell McInnes and Dorothy Silk sang Bach Cantatas and Purcell, and shivers went through everyone when Dorothy sang the still almost unknown *Blessed Virgin's Expostulation* with its piercing cries of 'Gabriel!', which Myra too had never heard before.

There were string quartets, clarinet quintets, and Myra played the Brahms and Franck piano quintets and many trios. One evening she began to play alone, on and on, whatever came into her mind or whatever was asked for. As the sun began to set through the west window, the moon began to rise through the east window, so that there was always just enough light. Groups of people sat on the floor, and even outside the open door, while the timeless stream of beauty flowed on. Then a late supper, and of course more laughter.

Myra's sense of balance was remarkable even in her youth. At a time when natural exuberance could, and occasionally did, over-ride her training, she was always ready to listen not only to her teacher and her fellow artists but even to her friends and pupils, and many of them will remember how often they heard the question after a concert: 'Was it a little better?' or 'Was it a little nearer the truth?' Naturally in these days there was a greater freedom of expression and of movement which gradually became more controlled; and also a note of passion, and even where appropriate of voluptuousness, which was often missing later; yet even then there was the almost classical instinct of 'Nothing too much'. Her beautifully clear and firm handwriting expressed this, and made it quite hard to throw away even an envelope!

Since she was sincerely seeking for truth it is not surprising that she became more and more sensitive to the finest shades of significance in whatever music she was playing, and it seemed that it was this attitude which so often allowed her to enter into its very heart and to unveil it to her audiences. She had what is so well expressed by that untranslatable German word, *Weihe*; and I remember my mother turning to me after an early performance and whispering, 'It is as if she were keeping a flame alight on the altar of music. . .' And indeed this was just what she was doing all her life, and almost literally so throughout the wartime National Gallery Concerts when its voice was so nearly stilled and that flame burned so low.

A tour in Holland in 1921 made one realize how greatly those audiences affected her. Her first real success had been there and she already had a devoted public, particularly in Amsterdam, where Willem Mengelberg was conductor of the Concertgebouw Orchestra. From earliest days she had established a happy relationship with both conductor and orchestra wherever she played, and as so often later they seemed all to inspire each other. Here the audience seemed to play a special part in it too, and a performance of the Grieg Concerto became a thing of high romance and poetry. 'Something happened', as she would say after a specially airborne performance. Even in later tours and with works of greater stature, these early concerts in Holland were hardly excelled, and for nearly fifty years she remained one of their most loved artists. Her Albert Hall concert in aid of Holland in the Second World War and her flight there in an R.A.F. plane before the country was fully liberated belong to another story.[1] But she recalled that when she opened her first concert with the Dutch National Anthem to an audience largely of service men, starving for this forbidden sound, and for all music, she was hardly able to go on playing. Probably never before and never again was she given such a clear revelation of music as living water, and the effect upon her was incalculable.

How clearly too her first visit to Italy stands out: waking up in the plain of Lombardy with the sun gilding the Alps, and Florence, Siena, Perugia and Assisi ahead. Her whole

[1] See p. 78: 'Anglo-Dutch Autumn', by Sir Paul Mason. (Ed.)

being seemed to be absorbing the new world of beauty as its natural nourishment. Everything she saw or heard went into that mysterious storehouse of heart and mind, to be sifted and matured, and finally translated into the language of music. This alchemy was almost tangible in those days. She looked at pictures, sculpture, country, cities with that same quality with which she listened to music: one of total receptiveness, fresh and untinged by pre-conceptions, and above all unblemished by self-assertion. She spent long times before the pictures which she loved best; not a word spoken, as though she was listening as well as looking, and with the same veiled and inward concentration which always enveloped her when she began to play. On reaching Assisi, and turning at the top of the hill to find the miraculous view over the valley below, she was breathing her own air and could hardly be torn away. By some re-arrangement she was able to stay on there for nearly a week and to watch the changing light and colour, walk in the hills, gaze at the Giotto frescos and absorb the still undisturbed magic of the whole place.

From there she went straight to Paris where a friend lent her a room, again with a little upright piano; there she worked every morning at the Beethoven G major Concerto, to lay deeper foundations for her lifelong communion with that work. Paris would be explored in the afternoons, and a clear memory is of her first sight in the Louvre of the Victory of Samothrace, for which no photograph had ever prepared her. She was quite literally overwhelmed by it, and spent long times drinking it in from all angles, often slipping in after the tourists had gone and 'letting it have its way' with her, listening to what it had to say.

Later visits to Venice and Rome were equally rewarding though never again could the impact of a first visit to Italy be quite repeated. She enjoyed the people and the life and the shops and the children every bit as much as the sight-seeing, and to her delight was quite often accepted as an Italian because of her appearance. Wherever there was a piano music was made and people would gather from no-where and listen to an impromptu recital, even the children spellbound. Language never seemed a barrier; wherever she went she made herself quickly and happily understood, for although she had a natural gift for foreign languages, no one could have spoken more naturally and more fluently the universal language of the heart.

In those years, too, no one who attended them can ever forget the two-piano recitals (called by their friends 'Myrenes') with her fellow pupil and lifelong friend Irene Scharrer;[1] these concerts were indescribably happy and brilliant, the quintessence of lovely and light-hearted music making. At some point in a concert there was sure to be a remark or a gesture by one or both of them which would convulse the audience, after which the Wigmore Hall be-came the scene of an enchanting family party, with count-less encores thrown off with the ease and grace of a fountain.

Myra loved the old Queen's Hall, and never ceased to miss it after its tragic destruction. Wherever she went she loved the atmosphere, the traditions, of great music and artists, and was always exceedingly sensitive to this; but her rever-ence for great traditions in no way diminished her reverence for great living artists, and all her life her attitude to these can perhaps best be described in the words of a Dutch friend: 'It is to kneel before'!

Her love of chamber music, which found such wide scope in the hundreds of chamber concerts she organized and often played in at the National Gallery, culminated after the war in the concerts with Casals at his Prades and Perpignan Festivals. Some of these performances, which were perhaps the crown of her musical life, have fortunately been recor-ded. The friendship with Casals was most deeply cherished, as were the many warm and mutually enriching friendships throughout her life. They are too many to enumerate, but one may mention the names of Harold Bauer, John Galsworthy, Benno Moiseiwitsch, Harold Samuel, Elena

[1] See p. 2: 'A Unique Friendship', by Irene Scharrer. (Ed.)

Gerhardt, Bruno Walter, John Masefield, and Stafford and Isobel Cripps.

Though she became the recipient of so many public honours, including some of the highest musical ones, she seemed never to get over the feeling of almost puzzled incredulity each time. But her acceptance of these honours always brought with it a deepened sense of responsibility as a servant of music and of the public.

Did Myra have no faults? How she would have repudiated and even rebuked the bare suggestion! Although genuinely grateful for any sincere appreciation, she was almost shocked by any kind of exaggeration. Yet if one tries to recall what these faults were it seems almost impossible to recapture them, so free was she from most of the usual ones, and so seemingly devoid of the seven deadly ones, though she made repeated claims to idleness and stupidity. These claims however failed remarkably to convince! But of course without a measure of shortcomings her sympathy and understanding, and her music, could never have been what they were, for she was above all things human. Apart from the countless people who were blessed by her music, there were many hundreds more who were also blessed personally by what a young man pupil called 'the healing quality of her loving-kindness'. Although she was the recipient of innumerable joys, sorrows, burdens or problems she always seemed to have time to listen and to share them. Again and again she was the first to be beside someone in need, even though her engagement book was full, and there might be a train to catch; and again and again it was she who went on caring far beyond the normal limits of human sympathy and help. It was always a marvel that she could combine such deep and continuous sympathy for so many people all over the world, with such unswerving dedication to music and to the gruelling demands of a public artist's life; and further, that in these widespread relationships, with every possibility of the wires crossing, such harmony was maintained. Her spiritual telephone exchange was supremely well run!

These were some of the ingredients of her nature when she set out alone on her first American tour, an experience which has daunted many mature artists. The long and brilliant story of these tours is told elsewhere, for they formed a great part of her life and inspiration.[1]

As time went on her programmes naturally changed. In the early years, besides the classics, she played a good deal more Schumann, Chopin, Brahms, Franck, Debussy, Ravel, Granados, de Falla and Albeniz. It is impossible to describe the luminous grace and poetry of some of these early performances, but a fair reminder can be heard in her recordings of Schumann's *Carnaval*, and even more in the Granados *La Maja y el Ruiseñor*. Several concertos were more rarely played, among them the Grieg and the Franck Symphonic Variations, while all five Beethovens, both Brahms, and all of the twenty-one Mozart Concertos emerged. Her love for these last was something quite apart and indescribable. She so felt the mystery and the underlying tragic quality, and so cherished some words of Bruno Walter when he was rehearsing Mozart: 'Il faut que ça soit si gai, si gai, que l'on ait envie de fondre en larmes. . .'

Her love for Schubert, always deep, steadily deepened with the years. As time went on she became more and more immersed in the late Beethoven Sonatas, especially the last three. Towards the end these became almost her musical Bible, and the last notes I ever heard her play were the *Andante* of Op. 109, when perhaps with some premonition, she took leave of our piano and kissed and thanked it.

Asked at that time what had been her ideal, the reply came without hesitation, unchanged after fifty years: 'To get a little nearer to the Truth'.

Can one doubt that this ideal has been fulfilled?

[1] See p. 27: 'American Pilgrimage', by Anita Gunn; p. 44: 'Myra in America' by Professor Bruce Simonds; and p. 38: 'Myra and her Audience' by Professor Arthur Mendel. (Ed.)

Myra and Uncle Tobs

BY

DENISE LASSIMONNE

---

*Musique! hôte total qui envahie sans qu'on discerne, qui
promet plus que l'amour . . .
Etre étonné c'est un Bonheur.*
ANNA COMTESSE DE NOAILLES

BOTH THESE epigrams might have been conceived to
epitomize Myra Hess, kindling the light of the star
which made her life a continual source of happiness
and fulfilment. Continuing to be astonished; continuing to
remain 'new' to the end in the presence of what is new; for
all is ever new to the pure in spirit.

That was one of the secrets of Myra's greatness, an
affinity she shared with her illustrious master and friend,
Tobias Matthay. They both possessed this gift. It permeated
their daily lives and their art, and proved a matchless
and enduring bond. The quest never ceased.

I had the privilege of witnessing this rare relationship,
since from early youth I was part of the Matthay household
at High Marley in Surrey. Myra often came to stay there,
and her visits were times of exceptional anticipation and
joy for 'Punkey', as she always called Tobias Matthay. At
the sound of her car hooting its way up the steep drive all
work was instantly dropped: there he stood at the front
door beaming with delight and quickly she was enfolded
in his warm embrace, to which extra comfort and security
were added by the special peaty smell emanating from the
old Irish tweeds that he wore in the country. Not a moment
was lost, but straight to the music-room and the piano,
where she must immediately hear a new composition of
his, or a new way of moulding a phrase in some well-known

17

work, and burning discussions would arise on technical problems while the hours fled by until someone came in to remind them gently that it was time for luncheon, and that Myra might be tired after her long drive. But no signs of tiredness reigned in that room: only two vivified and absorbed faces sharing the same interest and charged with happiness.

After these first overflowing moments, life resumed its accustomed course, which at High Marley generally meant each one to his regular work. But when we gathered together again, Myra's infectious laughter filled the house— she laughed with such warmth and, unlike most people, with the *whole* of herself. The speaking voice was in contrast withdrawn and of an exceptionally mellow and hauntingly tender quality. Her sense of fun brimmed over on to everything, and gaiety flowed from her being like a sparkling mountain torrent. Typical of this mischievous quality was an episode when Harold Samuel was adjudicating for a competition at the Tobias Matthay Pianoforte School. Myra decided to fool him by putting in her mouth a fearful set of protruding false teeth, wearing spectacles and letting down her hair. At the end of the competition she walked demurely in, handed Harold her number as all the other candidates had done, and proceeded to the piano. She then began to massacre one of the Bach Preludes and Fugues. He listened until he could decently stop her by saying, 'Thank you, that's enough.' At this point Myra lost her control. She burst out laughing, removed her spectacles and false teeth, and the two of them collapsed. The noise brought in Punkey and the rest; and when they looked at the mark-sheets it was discovered that Harold's comment on his latest candidate was, 'Not quite up to it!' She adored that sort of game, and easily became a naughty and very endearing little girl—a part of her nature that floated near the surface, and bubbled out at the least provocation.

Walks in that lovely hilly countryside were part of the day's enjoyment, and I can still vividly see Punkey and

Myra setting off arm in arm for 'a short trot'—never a long one, as Myra when I knew her was not a great walker and Punkey soon felt the ever-present urge to return to his demanding Muse.

He worked late into the night and scarcely ever retired before 2 a.m. Myra when staying with us nearly always played Patience[1] in the evening while we chatted—game after game until the early hours. On coming down from his study, Punkey would find her still sitting there for 'just one more game'. He would then vanish, to return shortly with apples, raisins and biscuits; and together they had their midnight feast.

Before giving a new recital programme, Myra always came down to Marley to go through the music with him. I remember a special occasion after one of these sessions when she said she would have a long practice; as I was then very young and loved Myra with veneration, but with considerable awe when it came to her music, I was all agog to hear *how* she practised, so sat down quietly on the other side of the music-room door with one ear glued to the keyhole. For a long time nothing happened, not a sound. Then there came the soft, soft playing over of a phrase. Again silence, until a few more quiet notes were experimented with. Once more silence. After a couple of hours of this she emerged—I had rushed away just in time—and with a look of complete satisfaction said, 'I have had *the* most wonderful practice.'

W. H. Davies begins one of his poems with these words—

> *What work is going on down underground*
> *Without a sound—without the faintest sound.*

The living reality had just been made manifest.

To us students practice meant playing passages over and over again—no wasting of time, etc.—and behold the greatest lesson, on *how* to work had been revealed—LISTENING and trying to reproduce what had been inwardly heard. Of

---

[1] Patience (Eng.) = Solitaire (Amer.). (Ed.)

course this was almost a final practice before a concert; but an immensity of knowledge had been passed on.

One of the points that Punkey insisted on as a last practice before playing in public was to go through the whole programme silently with the score in front of us—just as a conductor does—thereby keeping the mind alert and the ear fresh. No one fulfilled this principle more faithfully than Myra, and it is perhaps one of the fundamental reasons why her performances of works she played innumerable times always retained their freshness.

Punkey bequeathed another precious legacy to his pupils. Whenever he was with us in the artists' room, his last injunction before we stepped on the platform was '*Enjoy* the music!' That inspired phrase saved us from many possible disasters; and Myra used to say that when she suffered from nerves, as all great artists do, she would repeat to herself the magic words and a lifeline was cast and clung to, enabling her to throw herself into the very centre of the music shedding all nervousness in waste land.

Another recollection that comes to mind is of hearing Mr. and Mrs. Matthay reminiscing together over the early days of his many gifted young pupils. Myra was invariably singled out. He retraced her lessons, when she was calm and unruffled and would play so movingly that it pierced the heart. But when it came to the small regular practice concerts, she would go off the deep end. Then 'little Hess always bolted and lost control'—in fact, she became another person. This of course was in the dim past. Years of experience and deep musical awareness conquered all that, and brought a perfectly proportioned balance to her own great performances. She was no longer 'little Hess' but 'My Prophetess of Music', as was inscribed on one of his photographs given to her in later years.

It was while several of us were sitting on the terrace at High Marley during the early weeks of the war that Myra said she felt music should be given *daily* to the people of London, to make up for all the concerts that had so sud-

MYRA WITH TOBIAS MATTHAY JUST BEFORE HER
FIRST AMERICAN TOUR, 1922

MYRA WITH HER MOTHER

denly been stopped. There and then the National Gallery
Concerts were conceived. Some ten days later, with an
extremely premature birth, they first saw light. And they
lasted a full six and a half years, thanks to Myra's selfless and
unflagging devotion, gallantly helped by her wonderful and
courageous niece, Beryl Davis, and by her great friend, the
composer Howard Ferguson.

Wartime Christmases filled High Marley with friends,
Myra always among them. It was then that Punkey's great
moment came. He revelled in charades, or 'Dumb Crambo'
as he called it. He was the sole actor, and for weeks ahead
clothes disappeared from cupboards and utensils from the
kitchen: everything imaginable was collected. Once Christmas dinner was over the performance began. Syllable after
syllable was portrayed with great dramatic élan; and woe
betide us if the complete word was guessed too quickly!
The only *petit marmiton* allowed to join in was the dog,
who faithfully followed his master in and out of each act.
In the pre-war days, if Myra happened to be away on an
American tour she shared in these delicious pranks just the
same. Punkey never failed to write her about every word
he was going to use, with a detailed description of the scenes
he would act, and so made her feel she was participating
in the Christmas joys even though far away.

Their deep closeness and their thoughtfulness for each
other and for all who came within their orbit cast a sense
of sustenance, and an illuminative need to create and spread
goodness within one's measure. No mightier gift can be
handed to us mortals, and those two noble souls indeed
enriched the earth.

In the Twenties

BY

SIR STEUART WILSON

N O DOUBT one ought to keep a diary, or at any rate one ought to have kept one; these good intentions are renewed with each New Year, but seldom last beyond a few weeks. On the other hand alphabetical address books, though never dated, are seldom thrown away and my own dog-eared, pencil-scrawled book is still around and from its nature I guess that it dates from the First War, when I came in 1913 to live in London for the first time.

The first entry under 'H' is 'Hess, Myra, 8 Carlton Hill, N.W., Hamp. 1942'. I heard her play in the year 1912 or 1913 when she shared a recital at the Aeolian Hall with a young singer called Geoffrey Gwyther. I had heard him sing as an Oxford undergraduate on various occasions—I was myself at 'the other place' (not as now, 'an other place') and I had the same ambitions and wanted to see how they ever came to bear their first buds, if not fruit. Myra Hess played two groups, I don't remember them at all, but I remember most vividly the impression that this pleasant, assured, concentrated young pianist made upon me, a postulant at the threshold of the profession.

The Great War intervened and in 1920 I battered at the gates again. In January 1920 music suffered a grievous loss in the death of Gervase Elwes in a tragic accident in Boston, U.S.A., where he was giving a recital in his tour, and in February a small memorial concert was organized by André Mangeot at the Music Society's rooms in Westminster, at which the newly formed English Singers contributed some appropriate motets. I was asked to sing Vaughan Williams' 'On Wenlock Edge' which had been given its first performance by Gervase Elwes in 1909. As the result of this concert Myra asked me if I would take part in a concert which she was giving at the Wigmore Hall. The programme included a Concerto for piano by Arthur Bliss. It was in an unusual form because it included a tenor solo, treated as an instrument completing the ensemble, without words such as might convey a specific meaning, yet not a wordless *vocalise* in the manner of the composer's Rhapsody for wind, string quartet with soprano and tenor solo. It was as I said, 'wordless', but the composer wanted the sound of words without their connotations, so I provided a draft of such sentences, but a friend of Arthur's—whose name I no longer remember—had forestalled me. The piano part was of special interest because Myra, as an inveterate 'classicist', did not as a rule perform any contemporary music at all.[1] The Concerto was withdrawn and reappeared in a different guise as the Concerto for two pianos.

I heard her play to friends, but not at a concert, César Franck's *Prélude, Aria et Final* and I think she introduced me to a number of smaller organ or harmonium pieces; but so far as I remember the usual war-horse *Prélude, Choral et Fugue* was not then in her stable.

In the years 1923–5 I was in a temporary withdrawal myself owing to ill-health and two seasons of study with Jean de Reszke in France. Recovery and a return to the busy routine of a young singer's life did not bring me into personal touch with her again until, in 1929, I had the chance of a visit to the United States on a concert tour and in the course of this I met Myra in Boston. She gave me an introduction to her agent Annie Friedberg, who, for the next two or three seasons acted for me in the vain struggle to establish myself against the 'depression'. I sank into the vortex and was lost; Myra battled and won through to fame and success, but it was a real battle for her.

Later on we had few occasions for meeting and perhaps

[1] Myra did in fact play a considerable amount of contemporary music at that period. (Ed.)

only on the issues which then swayed the Incorporated Society of Musicians, which took a strong line on permits for foreign artists. Myra had been a regular visitor to the U.S.A. rather than Europe and felt that she could not, from that position, attempt to impose any limits to their artists coming over here, while we were free, and indeed welcomed, as regular migrants to their climate.

Finally in 1946 at the end of the series of National Gallery Concerts, Frank Howes organized a dinner at the Savoy in her honour, as a mark of appreciation for all she had done for us musicians. I was, at that time, Music Director of the Arts Council and had the privilege of voicing the gratitude of the large company that assembled and of speaking for the profession of music which had been given so splendid an opportunity, and for the Musicians Benevolent Fund which benefited by more than £16,000. Frank Howes had decided that it was to be on 'Gala Scale', white ties, white waistcoats, decorations and all the trimmings of the return to normal life. It was a strain on the wardrobe of many of us, when bombs and moth had done their worst, and we all noticed the pervading bouquet of camphor which marked the reappearance of many treasures.

Myra was at all times, and especially in our youth, the greatest fun and amusing company. One of her special parlour tricks was her pose as Queen Victoria with a lace-edged handkerchief as a widow's cap. Once, it is said, that she and Harold Samuel were discovered prone on the lid of a grand piano to see if they could play duets upside-down!

Conducting for Myra

BY

SIR ADRIAN BOULT

IT SO happens that Dame Myra Hess was one of the first pianists with whom I came in professional contact: when the 1914 War was just drawing to an end. The work was the Schumann Concerto at Holloway Polytechnic Theatre on 9 March 1918, and I was, of course, captivated by it all. I remember thinking, too, that if I always had soloists like that to accompany in concertos I should be a very happy man.

Since that time there have been countless occasions when I have had the privilege of working with her. In particular I cannot forget two concerts in which we were joined at the piano by a great friend of both of us, Harold Samuel. The programme consisted of three double concertos, two by Bach and one by Mozart, and practically nothing else. I think the first occasion was in London, but it was repeated in Birmingham, and they invited me to repeat it again in New York, but unfortunately this fell through for some reason. I particularly remember the Birmingham occasion when the audience was literally spellbound, and at the end of the concert we had to repeat the last movement of the Bach C major.

Again she used to come to some very notable concerts that were given at the Petersfield Musical Festivals. Until the Town Hall was built they took place in a very decrepit drill hall where the heating was intense and seating most uncomfortable; but besides the audience, which consisted partly of Hampshire county and partly of people who came up from Portsmouth, there was always a Choir of something like 200, who belonged to small choral societies from villages

25

whose names were quite unknown except to inhabitants of the neighbourhood. The Festival Day for members of these societies would sometimes last as long as 18 to 20 hours, for there would be a milk-round or something before coming down to the 9.30 a.m. competitions, and they would stay for the afternoon and evening, singing as members of the combined choir in a great choral work of Bach, Beethoven or Brahms. These people were the ideal audience, and it was a wonderful thing to look up and see the faces of these humble choral singers and realize how much the music meant to them, and how much they appreciated what a great artist like Myra Hess could give them.

More recently I remember the occasion in the autumn of 1952 when the London Philharmonic Orchestra asked her to play the five Beethoven Concertos with us in four concerts at the Royal Festival Hall. The performances were most impressive, for no one could convey the artistic development and style through the five concertos with greater effect than Dame Myra; and at the end of it I was immensely touched to receive from her a copy of *The Life of George V* with the following inscription: 'This book, with my love and gratitude, seals the importance of No. 5. To Adrian from Myra.'

Finally I conducted for Myra at the Festival Hall on 31 October 1961 at what was to be her last appearance in public, though neither I nor anyone else realized this sad fact at the time. The concert was in remembrance of the 21st Anniversary of the Battle of Britain, and the concerto she played was the Mozart in A major, K.488.

I see from my records that there were altogether twenty-one performances of Beethoven No. 4 and ten performances of the Schumann, including one at The Hague on 19 October 1955. There were, of course, many others but none in which I did not feel somehow the better for the contact with her. Her unflinching idealism seemed to affect everything around her, and literally inspired not only her own playing, but that of everyone connected with her.

American Pilgrimage

BY

ANITA GUNN

YRA'S CAREER in America, which was destined to span nearly forty years, began with an Intimate Recital in Steinway Hall on 12 January 1922 before a small audience of musicians. On 17 January she gave her first New York recital at the Aeolian Hall. A great deal depended on it, as the New York critics, such as Richard Aldrich of the *New York Times* and many others of the first rank, could make or mar a reputation all over the country. The whole enterprise of her coming to America had been a venture and the *deus ex machina* who had brought it about was César Saerchinger. He was a mutual friend of Myra and Annie Friedberg, the concert manager, and he convinced the one that there was a future for her in America and persuaded the other to break her rule of never taking an artist she had not heard—and a notoriously unsaleable commodity at that—a woman pianist.

The morning after that first recital Annie was up at cockcrow to see the reviews, and when, in person, she woke Myra from a sound sleep some hours later, she was heavily veiled to hide the fact that she had been crying with sheer excitement. The notices were wonderful. In spite of the difficulties, Annie had booked Myra a big tour taking her right across the country to California and, with the New York press behind her, hope rose high. The press was a help, but the secret of Myra's success from then on lay in herself, her consummate art, and her approach to music. She never played down to an audience in any way; a small town in Nebraska would be given the same choice of programme as was New York, and in a land where audiences were rather

27

used to being swept off their feet by towering virtuosi, they were completely won over by the atmosphere of intimate music making that she created the minute she walked on to the platform. She made them feel that they were all there to hear and enjoy beautiful music, with no hint of exhibitionism. It was this, together with her unswerving integrity in the choice of programmes, that gave the unique quality to the position she was always to hold in America. Of course, it grew with the passing years, but the foundation was laid on that first tour.

It was an arduous business, travelling alone—and travelling was travelling in those days, when air-conditioning had not been invented and it took five days to get from New York to California. Her success everywhere was immediate. She played with orchestra in Philadelphia, San Francisco, Minneapolis, and with the New York Philharmonic under Mengelberg and the Boston Orchestra in Cambridge under Pierre Monteux.

In spite of the burden of doing all her own packing and correspondence, the worst thing she had to combat was overwhelming home-sickness; but she had already made friendships that were to be life-long. Foremost among these were with Frederick and Julia Steinway, two aristocrats of the musical life of New York, whose home was a focal point for all artists; they took 'Little Hess' to their hearts at once. The last concert of the tour was on 9 April 1922 and she returned home with the knowledge that her future in America was assured.

The following few excerpts from the press show something of the impact made by her playing in the early years:

New York Times; Richard Aldrich: 'There was strangely little temptation to consider what kind of pianist Myra Hess is at her appearance at Aeolian Hall, to analyse how she is doing this or that, what sort of "reading" she was giving, what technical procedures she was going through, what the nature of the artistic personality was that was accomplishing

the performances. There was a constant invitation to delight
in the music itself, to listen to it, to find in it the sole and
sufficient purpose and end of the evening. . . There are not
many such evenings to be passed at Aeolian or any other hall
in the course of a season and it might be argued that there
are not many artistic achievements of the same sort, so complete so finished in their way.'

New York World; Deems Taylor: 'After Myra Hess had
finished the printed programme at her recital last night we
caught five licenced music critics standing in the rear of
Aeolian Hall waiting to hear her first encore. Why they
waited, we cannot, of course, know with any certainty, but
we have an idea they had forgotten to be critics and wanted
to hear some more music . . . she plays like a musician and
artist; and that means, as it generally does, that her technical
equipment is perfect enough to be taken for granted. . . One
may not agree with her interpretation of a particular work.
But anything she does has intelligence, sincerity and understanding behind it. And so it is better than correct, it is
beautiful.'

Ohio State Journal: 'A capacity house and enthusiastic
applause greeted what was by far the finest music that the
Cleveland Orchestra's Columbus performances has given this
year. . . One number stood out so far above all others, so
rarely with such jewel-like loveliness, that it must take first
place. This was the Mozart Concerto in D minor. . . To Myra
Hess is due praise of such high quality that one longs for one
of her own perfectly made phrases with which to express it.'

Her second tour started in January 1923 and was so successful, that she went back again in the October of that
year. From now on, her American tours became annual
events, with her reputation growing steadily. At first Annie
Friedberg was a little doubtful of Myra's *modus vivendi;*
her abhorrence of publicity, her avoidance of big social entertainment, the fact that she usually wore black on the
platform and that nothing would induce her to put 'popular

numbers' in her programmes. But gradually she came to trust Myra's instinct and even agreed that her fee should not be raised to the extent that was justified by her success. There were many places where Myra loved playing, such as universities that could not afford high fees, and she preferred the quality of her audience to the amount of money she made. They were very wise, as Myra was one of the few artists who did not have to lower her fee and thereby, her prestige, when the depression came.

I first travelled with Myra in 1931, by which time her name was fast becoming a household word and in lifts and suchlike places I often had to hiss 'Look out, you're becoming famous,' as one saw recognition dawning in someone's eye. Throughout the years her routine remained unaltered; arrived at a place, she would go straight to the hall to try the piano and if possible, do a couple of hour's work— no dinner before the concert and if there was a party after, it would be an informal one. In spite of this, her vivid personality, her unaffected friendliness and sparkling sense of humour won her friends wherever she went and as her tours took her from end to end of the country, they soon numbered legion.

By now she was appearing regularly with the major orchestras and those years were studded with unforgettable musical experiences: as on the occasion when she played the Brahms D minor Concerto with the Detroit Orchestra under Gabrilowitsch. The work was in their bones, as Gabrilowitsch often played it with them without a conductor and, great artist that he was, he gave Myra the accompaniment of a life-time. In 1925 she first played the Beethoven 4th Concerto with Koussevitzky and the Boston Orchestra, the beginning of a long series of performances of that work in which they felt especially as one. Soon after this she played with them every year and when in 1933 she was soloist for their Pension Fund Benefit, they gave her an inscribed silver bowl that was to remain one of her most cherished possessions.

An incident with a lighter touch was in 1937, when she was engaged to play for the Ford Hour, for an astronomic fee for those days, the 1st movement of the Grieg Concerto and a group of solos. The rehearsal was fairly hair-raising, with everything timed to a split second, so that not a moment of time 'on the air' should be wasted; but she did not realize how little margin there was, before the evening. Owing to the feeling of tension, she had a stupendous attack of pre-concert nerves and shut herself into the sitting room of the suite she had booked on the strength of the fee, and went on practising until far too late. When she tried to emerge, she found the lock had jammed and there she was. In view of the colossal importance of not being a minute late at the hall, it was rather a shattering moment. However, our combined strength finally got it open and she dressed with the speed of a quick-change artist and just made it. She was escorted to a little gilt chair on the stage while the overture was being played and when it was over, she started for the piano. To her horror, she had only taken a couple of steps when she heard the drum-roll starting the Concerto—she made one dive for the keyboard and played the first chord standing up! After the concert was over, she danced up to an astonished policeman on duty backstage and told him that no-one had any right to the amount of money she was being paid. Actually, she felt she had earned every penny.

By 1939 Myra was on the crest of the wave of popularity. She was in demand all over the country, with more engagements than she could take, and the tour planned for the autumn was to have been the most extensive yet, followed by a visit to Honolulu and Australia. Why she cancelled on the outbreak of war has been told elsewhere, but she had a difficult time.[1] For once, Annie's imagination failed her and she could see no larger issues than a contract to be honoured. She felt, and said forcibly, that Myra's career in America would be finished and that there could be no justification for her staying in England, when so many English artists

[1] See p. 90: 'The National Gallery Concerts and After'. (Ed.)

were still coming over to the States. Feeling that in the circumstances Annie could not handle the publicity in the right way, Myra put it all into the hands of Anita Chase, her manager in Boston, whose imaginative sympathy gave her a clear grasp of the whole situation.

When the National Gallery Concerts finally ended in 1946, Myra planned her return to America for the autumn of that year and a short but representative tour was arranged. She was bound to wonder what this gap of seven years would mean in a country where the emphasis on piano playing had swung greatly towards technical virtuosity, with the fabulous generation of pianists that had grown up in the meantime. In New York, Myra found that even the action of Steinway pianos had changed to a lightness that disconcerted her. What would the audiences, used to speed and brilliance, think of her very different playing?

The answer came at her first recital that took place in Town Hall, New York. Annie had urged her to move to Carnegie Hall, but Myra insisted that she would return as she had left; because of the lack of clothing coupons, she even wore the same dress she had for her last concert in 1939. The story of her work during the war had fired the imagination of the American people and when she walked on to the stage for that first concert, the packed house stood to welcome a beloved friend. At the end they stood again and the ovation was even greater, for they found that her art had grown and flowered in the years of trial and stress; a new dimension was there, together with all the old magic. In the interval, Myra made a speech in which she expressed her gratitude for the American and Canadian help that had enabled the Gallery Concerts to continue through the Blitz, when they were given in a small air-raid shelter, and she also touched on wider issues. To quote a critic who paraphrased the speech: 'It would not be easy to match the simplicity and warmth of her words, nor is it even possible to give more than an indication of the effect, for example, of the mystical Sonata Opus 110 of Beethoven as she played

it yesterday with all imaginable intimacy and inner feeling. . .'

So many people had been turned away from this first
recital, that Myra was persuaded to give a second in Carnegie
Hall at the end of the tour. It was announced and sold out
in a single day. The whole tour developed into a triumphal
progress; each place seemed to vie with the others in paying
her honour. In Washington, President Truman came to
meet and hear her when she played with the National
Orchestra and there was a big reception for her at the British
Embassy; in Chicago the Orchestra stood when she came on
to the stage, while the brass section played a fanfare. She
played four times with the Boston Orchestra under Koussevitzky, in Providence, New York, Brooklyn and Boston,
where a large Dinner was given in her honour attended by
all the important people in the City. Perhaps the highlight
was her concert with Toscanini. It had been arranged that
she should play the Emperor Concerto with him and she
had been working furiously at it, whilst preparing the 4th
Beethoven for the concerts with Koussevitzky. She suddenly
had the feeling that Toscanini was tired of the Emperor
which everyone seemed to do with him, so she suggested
the 3rd Beethoven Concerto. He was delighted with the
change, but meanwhile Myra had to get the Emperor (on
which she had been concentrating so hard) out of her system
and work at the C minor—all this while she was playing
No. 4 nearly every night. She went to the famous 8H studio
from which Toscanini did all his broadcasting, for a piano
rehearsal and it was a revelation to discover his approach
to a work he must have known backwards. She found he
had already had three orchestral rehearsals without her;
there were two discussions with the piano alone and finally
two full-scale rehearsals with orchestra. Also, to her profound relief, he showed the uttermost respect for her interpretation and tempi—she had been trying to speed it up in
deference to what he was reputed to like. It is always moving
to be in the presence of greatness, especially when it is

coupled with the humility of genius. With Toscanini, as
with Myra, the inner vision so far exceeded what was in
fact attainable, that they were neither of them ever content
with a performance. After the concert, which was broadcast
from coast to coast, there was a supper at Toscanini's house.
The fare was sumptuous, but all the host ate was a little
soup and brown bread. It was the first of many evenings
spent in his inspiring company.

The tour was a tremendous artistic and personal triumph,
but short though it was, it made great demands on her.
Emotionally it was deeply moving and the fact that she spoke
in nearly every place she visited added enormously to the
inevitable tension. The press everywhere was enthusiastic.
Indeed all the critics seemed to agree with an eminent musi-
cologist in Indianapolis, about whom there was a nice story,
though the incident did not happen till a year or so later.
At a picnic supper after her concert, he asked Myra if he
could get her anything; she said 'Thank you, but I think
I've got everything.' Quick as a flash came his answer:
'You're telling me.'

Myra's tours once more became annual events and her
position in America was unique. Whenever she played with
orchestra it seemed to turn into a Myra Hess Festival, as
when she played six Mozart Concertos in Chicago, the entire
programmes being given over to those works. There were
three concerts in four days—the first programme being repeated next day and three different concertos one day later.
In San Francisco she played six times with the Orchestra
and gave a recital all within a calendar month, each time
to a sold-out Opera House. A surprising achievement in a
city with so comparatively small a population.

Soon after her return, she revived the practice, started
during the war, of using her score when she felt like it,
both in concerto and in recital. She wondered if it would
sound the death knell of her reputation, but such was her
status that something which had not been done in living
memory was accepted without criticism, and almost without

comment except for a vague feeling of disappointment when she chose to play from memory. The number of concerts each year was now limited and travelling was kept as much within bounds as possible. Myra's friend Dorothy Shepard, with her genius for organization and detail, laid a magic carpet of comfort over the U.S. railway system.

Annie Friedberg was now getting very old and though she indomitably carried on her work, she really was not up to it. César Saerchinger was in New York and Myra arranged that he should work in Annie's office, with special reference to her affairs. When Annie died in 1952, he took over the Management and Myra had many happy years of sympathetic work with him, his wife Marion, and the incomparable Lillian Knapp, who had been Annie's secretary and stayed on with the newly designated Friedberg Management. Thus was the cycle completed.

Myra's life was enriched by many new friends as well as the old. The House of Steinway was still her tower of strength, with Julia until her death in 1958, Sascha Greiner, and the unique 'Uncle Billy'. Later the younger generation were to play their part in this long association, Henry and Polly, Fritz and Johnnie.

Myra had often met Helen Keller, that great woman who so remarkably surmounted her blindness and deafness, through her friends Katherine Cornell and Nancy Hamilton, and one day Nancy asked if she could bring Helen to the hotel to hear Myra play. It was all arranged, but Myra wondered what kind of music it should be. Should it be percussive, so that Helen might more easily pick up the pulse and rhythm? However, she decided to leave it and sense what would be best. From the first note there was no doubt. As Myra started playing Helen began to conduct, following every nuance and inflection as well as the main content of the music. Her face was radiant and it was obvious that she lived every note with Myra. How this miracle was achieved, what sixth sense enabled her to 'hear', no one will ever know, but it was an incredibly moving hour.

Another good friend was Main Bocher, the famous New York couturier, who during her first post-war tour created a wonderful concert dress for her as a tribute, the first of many he was to make. Then there was an evening spent at Ronald Colman's fabulous house in Beverly Hills during a holiday Myra spent in California, when she played till the small hours, with at one juncture Douglas Fairbanks junior singing the orchestra part of a Brahms Concerto. There was too, a wonderful day with her beloved and revered friend Bruno Walter in his home, where they tried through Mozart Concertos for a concert in New York. Every time they played together was an experience that knitted their friendship ever more closely. She was deeply touched when the Royal Philharmonic Society asked her to receive their Medal on his behalf, when he was too ill to come to England.

The affection in which she was held everywhere, was underlined on many occasions, such as when she had an emergency gall-bladder operation in Chicago. Not only did the manager of the hotel, Otto Eitel, insist that from the moment she was taken ill, both she and I were his guests, but all radio programmes were changed and her records broadcast throughout the morning of the operation. Again, when she found that her 70th birthday would be spent in Washington without a concert, she said 'Good—no-one will know it is my birthday.' She could not have been more mistaken. Once again all radio stations put out important programmes about her, and there did not seem to be a person in the city who did not make some gesture.

After the first post-war recital in Town Hall, she moved finally to Carnegie Hall, realising that the vastly better acoustics more than justified the change. During these latter years those recitals were unique occasions. They were always sold out to the last standee, and when she walked on, a great wave of affection and anticipation rose to meet her like a tangible thing. In 1954 she played for the first time a programme that was to be for most people the peak of her interpretative achievement—the last three Beethoven Sonatas, Op. 109, 110 and 111. She had worked towards this for many years, including these works in other programmes, but it was not until she felt she was ready did she play them all together. It was something that no one who heard it is ever likely to forget. She seldom played any encores at the end, feeling that the last word must lie with the great C minor, and her audiences always seemed to agree; they wanted no lesser work to break the spell. These were the works she chose for her recital in 1960, when she thought that Carnegie Hall was to be demolished, and she wanted to pay tribute to its great tradition. The building was reprieved and she had planned to hail its future in 1961 with the same programme. But it was not to be, as illness cut short her tour and also prevented her ever going to America again. So the pilgrimage of nearly forty years ended, but the memory of her music will not soon be forgotten nor will her place be filled. It had not been an easy victory, and it came about through unswerving dedication and sacrifice, an integrity that scorned all compromise, and a devotion to the music that became the expression of a brilliant and vivid personality, pervaded with a deep love of humanity. It is no wonder that her position was unique and that with her passing a light has gone in the world.

Myra and her Audience

BY

ARTHUR MENDEL

O F ALL the performers I have heard, two stand out in my memory as having had an essential musicality different from all the rest: Fritz Kreisler and Myra Hess. There are still phonograph records of Kreisler's playing which young musicians who never heard him find musical in a unique way. I doubt that any of Myra's records will convey to future generations what we found unique in her.[1]

Why is this? I used to think that in the pieces she played best—the Bach G major French Suite, the Brahms Intermezzi and B minor Capriccio, the Schumann Concerto, the Beethoven Fourth, Opus 110, and (yes) 'Jesu, Joy of Man's Desiring'—she succeeded better than any other musician I knew in putting the listener in direct contact with the music. She was so completely, so unerringly musical that it seemed to me that she became the instrument through which the music realized itself. But with the best will in the world one rarely hears this in the records. Why? Were we really taken in by the spell of her personality? It was certainly true of her, as of Kreisler, that her bodily movements in playing seemed at the very least never to contradict the implicit gestures of the music, seemed indeed to grow out of them and enact them with extraordinary perfection. Were they so appropriate visually—was she in such large part the dancer—that we imagined the embodiment of these gestures in actual sound to be more successful than it really was? At best, recordings are of course a distortion of the sound of a living performance, and Myra's

---

[1] A striking exception, for which I do not know any explanation, is her recording of the Beethoven Sonata in E major, Op. 109.

discs were not examples of the best techniques of recording and manufacture even in their own day.

But the recordings of other artists, many other artists, including those of many years ago, come far closer to evoking the impression one had from their living performance than Myra's do.

She hated recording—but so do many performers. Yet I think that gives us a clue. For me another clue lies in the fact that in the many times I heard her play in private she never seemed to approach the quality of her greatest public performance. I think she was *essentially* a public performer. I think performance for her was *essentially* communication to an audience. She could not succeed in imagining an audience at the other end of a chain of electro-mechanical connecting links: microphone—amplifier—tape—disc—stylus—amplifier—loudspeaker. In saying this, I do not mean to be voicing either praise or blame, or to imply that other performers are less great because they do not look upon performance as direct communication with an audience. I mean that for better or worse the best in Myra had to be challenged by an audience physically present, and that the moment she lived for was that in which she felt the triumph of achieving communication to people who at all other moments were by comparison strangers to her.

When in the last years illness put an end to such triumphs, she was bereft. I confess that this troubled me; that I entertained superior thoughts about how she must have known that this moment of enforced retirement would probably come to her as it does to most performers, and how she should have prepared herself for it. I thought I understood that when one has been greeted with rapturous applause by thousands of people perhaps fifty times in the year it must be hard to face the fact that one is never going to have such a greeting again. But I thought she ought to be able to find enough to absorb her interests in the music she had never had time to study, the kind of study she had never had time to do, the pupils she had never had time to teach, and so on.

Only now, when I try to analyse what was unique about the musical experience I owe to her, does it strike me that the release of that spark that flew from her to her audience in her highest moments must have been an experience of such intensity that no other in life could approach it. And that it is to the very narrowness that made this relation to an audience the one thing in life that really mattered that we owe the intensity of musical experience that she uniquely gave us. So only now do I think I understand the emptiness in her life during those last sad years when she felt she had lost that contact with us compared to which any other was meaningless—though many of us all over the world will not altogether lose contact as long as we live with the musical experience she made us alive to.[1]

To try to analyse what made her playing unique is frustrating—since in a sense it can all be summed up by saying that it simply lacked anything clumsy, anything literal, anything arbitrary, anything unmusical. This seems faint praise until one remembers how literally true it is, and how different hers was from almost any other performance one has known. Notes *never* were separate entities in her playing; they were always parts of a process, like the individual 'still' frames of motion-picture film, always organic parts of a phrase, a musical gesture. Other performers achieve the perfectly musical gesture occasionally; she, it seemed, never had to achieve it—she could not avoid it. The phrase took its place perfectly in the larger framework of the whole piece, but it was the perfection of the shaping—rhythmic, dynamic, colouristic—of each phrase that came forth from her that seems to me what she shared with Kreisler and with no one else in my experience. I think particularly of the crescendo and the rubato near the end of the Brahms

---

[1] I think Professor Mendel's explanation is mistaken. He did not know of the physical causes when he wrote. See p. 103 of 'The National Gallery Concerts and After'. (Ed.)

Capriccio, which I always thought I remembered clearly; and yet whenever I heard her play it again I had to realize that what I had remembered was hardly more than a caricature of the subtlety of her playing. Or of the crescendo and diminuendo on the chord of G major that immediately precedes the inversion of the fugue in Op. 110, as wonderful in its way as the singing unity into which her playing moulded the simultaneous offbeat diminutions and augmentations of the fugue-subject on the next page.

When one heard music-making of this sort, one had the impression not that Myra was playing music, but that music was playing her.

I think one often has a similar impression with Bach: that he did not so much compose a piece like the third movement of the First Brandenburg, say, as discover it; that the statue already existed somehow in all its perfection and he only had to chip the marble away from around it. If one then looks at what he did with this movement in adapting it for the Cantata *Vereinigte Zwietracht der wechselnden Saiten*, one can see the actual process of reshaping—one can, to change the figure, watch the wheels go round. No question but what a fully conscious and purposeful intellect chooses the tracks upon which those wheels shall run; and no question, either, that an unerring instinct has laid out the tracks from among which the choice is made.

I had a striking demonstration once of the extent to which Myra consciously played the music which, as I have said, seemed really to play her.

When she returned to America in August 1946, after an absence of seven years, her closest American friends met her at the boat and took her home to dinner, where my wife and I joined them—an almost tearfully joyful reunion of the five of us. After dinner, she sat at the piano and played us the programme with which she was about to resume her American career. It began with the G major French Suite, which she played, as always, with matchless sensitivity, grace, and verve. In those days I was much more confident than I am now that I knew just how the ornaments should be played. So when Myra had gone off to the country for a rest preparatory to beginning her tour, I took my courage in both hands and wrote her a letter about the French Suite. Of course, I wrote her, I would rather hear her play it with her nineteenth-century style of ornament realization than anyone else play it with every appoggiatura in place. But why should she cling to old habits when we now knew better, why should she not begin her trills on the upper note, etc. I even made bold to write out approximations of how I thought some of the ornaments should go. In reply I had a cheery post-card from the country, thanking me for my pains and saying 'We must talk about these things one day', which I took to be a gentle way of dismissing me.

The recital at Town Hall in October was an Occasion: Myra resuming contact with her adoring American public. The moment when she sat down to play, after the cheering audience had held her standing for several minutes, was filled with anticipation that was tangible almost to the point of pain. It was not the moment one would have chosen as the likeliest for a demonstration of the details of *Aufführungspraxis*. But what followed the first three notes in the right hand of the Allemande of the G major Suite was— ever so delicately underlined and accompanied by the merest suggestion of a sidelong glance—not a c but a d. All four trills of those first four measures had been reshaped; my cup was full. Then she went back for the repeat, and now all the trills were as she had always played them. And so it went through the entire Suite: first time through, every repeated section with the ornaments as if straight out of Dolmetsch; second time in the good old-fashioned way. (Incidentally, the most knowledgeable newspaper critic the next day commented only on how 'prettily' Dame Myra had played the ornaments.) It was a characteristically witty and teasing reply to my missionary attempt, but what struck me most was the degree of conscious control that it showed, on an occasion when one might have imagined that more

than ever Myra might have let the music 'play her'. Needless to say, both sets of ornament-realizations had been
shaped by that unfailing musicality so that the choice was
not between a stiff and lifeless 'correctness' and an irresis-
tibly musical wrongheadedness, but between alternatives
both of which had been considered and felt.

We cannot bring Myra back. We cannot ever experience
that incomparable pianistic singing and dancing again. And
the words with which we try to conjure up our memories
of it have meaning, I dare say, only to those to whom they
are superfluous.

Myra in America

BY

BRUCE SIMONDS

O NE DAY in 1920, when I was a student in London, looking at the bulletin-board of the Tobias Matthay Pianoforte School on Wimpole Street, I saw the advance notice of a concert by Myra Hess. The photograph attracted me. There was a suggestion of latent power in the firm mouth of the youthful face, some mystery in the dark eyes, a hint of humour. From the catalogue of the school I had already seen that this person was one of Matthay's first assistant teachers and I decided to go to her recital in Queen's Hall on the 25th of September. The programme was devoted entirely to Chopin; of this she was incredulous, many years later. When the afternoon arrived a young woman in a pale blue gown appeared on the platform, approached the piano with a lithe, almost athletic step (how comfortably one reached the stage at Queen's Hall through that level curving corridor!) and began the seldom-played Chopin Prelude in C sharp minor, Op. 45; my attention was caught at once by her sensitive delivery of the opening phrase. She proceeded with the Barcarolle, the B flat minor Sonata and other compositions including the Mazurka in A minor, Op. 68 No. 2, which I have never seen on a programme since. I was enthralled, but a few days later when I spoke of my admiration to Mrs. Matthay she said thoughtfully 'Yes, but you have not heard the real Myra Hess yet.'

In those days Myra Hess's repertoire embraced music with which one does not associate her. Who would believe that she played the Mackenzie Scottish Concerto and even the piano part of Scriabin's *Prometheus*? Of course she played

44

these things because she was asked to do so, and as a young
artist she could not afford to neglect opportunities, but even
at that time she refused to play music which she considered
really inferior. Her predilections for Bach, Mozart, Beethoven, Schubert and Schumann appeared later. Her pre-
ference for music which was not mere glitter was illustrated
by the programme of her first New York recital on 17th
January, 1922. This began quietly with a tranquil Scarlatti sonata in C minor, continued with two more Scarlatti
pieces, the Bach Prelude and Fugue in B flat major from
the first book of the *Well-Tempered Clavier*, Franck's *Prélude, Aria et Final*, Schumann's *Papillons*, five pieces by
Debussy, the Nocturne in C minor and Polonaise in A flat
of Chopin. This was a singularly modest programme of
expressive but not especially brilliant music; and her appearance was equally modest, for to the horror of her manager
she chose to dress in black. In her later years she wore
black exclusively, sometimes with a dash of scarlet, and no
ornament whatever except a very beautiful jade pendant
which I think for her served as a kind of amulet.

This first recital evoked panegyrics from the experienced
and usually unimpressionable New York critics. The three
leading newspapers gave her what would now be called
'rave' notices. Richard Aldrich began his article in the *New
York Times* without circumlocution by calling her 'an extraordinary artist . . . one whose achievements gave all the
more pleasure for their unexpectedness.' Continuing, he
wrote 'She is a true interpreter; and makes her interpretat-
ions deeply engrossing through their vitality, their finesse and
subtle qualities, their intensity and glowing warmth. Her
technique is of a high development and is wholly under
her control. It is indeed of an uncommon brilliancy and
security even in these days of brilliant and secure technique;
but it does not shine as such, because it is wholly devoted
to the true uses of technique as a means of interpretation.
Her tone is clear, pure, delicately and warmly coloured; her
touch has variety of quality, power and force, and in its

lighter manifestations is delightful in its crispness . . . It may truly be said that there was an aristocratic distinction in her playing . . . as well as a rich gusto and a singular power of identifying herself with the many different styles involved, and setting forth each piece in its own distinctive and essential spirit.'

H. E. Krehbiel said in the *New York Tribune* 'Miss Hess comes bearing a beautiful message. None of our visitors has brought a more beautiful one . . . She is every inch an artist. . . She possesses not only fancy, but the higher gift which is imagination. Her expositions are not merely intellectual, they are poetical also.' With W. J. Henderson of the *New York Herald*, these critics were especially appreciative of her playing of the Schumann *Papillons*, which according to Mr. Aldrich 'glowed and glittered under her hands. Their graphic picturesqueness, their varying moods, their gaiety, tenderness, yearning boisterousness are a genuine expression of the flood of Schumann's earliest romantic spirit poured out in music; and as they are in the music, they were delightfully reproduced in Miss Hess's playing.' The Bach, Debussy and Chopin also elicited high praise.

In spite of these eulogistic notices, her reputation made its way slowly in America and her chance to attract a wider audience among the élite of music-lovers (there were only eighty-six people at her first recital) came in September 1923 when she was asked to play at Mrs. Coolidge's Pittsfield festival, presenting the Brahms viola sonata in F minor, the Bax sonata and Rebecca Clarke's Rhapsody with Lionel Tertis. It was a formidable ordeal to appear on the same programme with Katherine Goodson who had long been beloved in America, but she came through with flying colours. From then on her success was assured and her tours expanded to cover the whole territory of the United States and Canada from the Atlantic to the Pacific seaboard. She endured these exhausting journeys with remarkable stamina; but I doubt if she could have accomplished them then without the constant sympathetic companionship of Anita Gunn.

Her appearance on the platform had much to do with her success. Without mannerisms, serene and poised, she radiated an air of modest assurance and absorption in the music; no one could have guessed that she suffered agonies of nervousness before each performance. As it was, she subjugated her audience before she had played a note. Not really a beautiful woman by Hollywood standards, she seemed so on the stage; with a superb aquiline profile; taller than she really was; and though quiet in manner, sufficiently dramatic. She could have been a great actress.

My own acquaintance with her deepened when she began to play in New Haven, as she did every year for many years. In the intimate atmosphere of Sprague Hall which seats only 700 the qualities of her performance were shown at their best: her beautiful unforced tone, her rhythmic spontaneity, delicate shading and lack of sentimentality. Jordan Hall in Boston was another sympathetic environment. She did not really enjoy playing in the vast auditoriums so common in America.

As I came to know her better I became aware that her graciousness to others concealed a strong critical sense which applied to herself became ruthless and ferocious. This was particularly brought to my attention one day when she was staying at my house. She was at the end of a long and strenuous tour during which she had played the Brahms-Handel Variations everywhere, and she was to play them again that evening. After lunch she sat down to practise the Variations; I went out and returning an hour and a half later found her still practising them at a snail's pace, not having reached the final variations or the fugue. With her pupils she was equally demanding. After having kept one of my colleagues an hour on the first line of the Appassionata slow movement she remarked 'I have asked nothing of you today that I do not do myself every day of my life.' This slow meticulous practice she referred to, with a wry smile, as 'donkey-work'.

For all this intensity was enlivened by a constant sense

of humour. As I was lunching one day alone in a New York restaurant a pencilled scrap of paper was brought to me by the waiter. Mystified for a moment I read:

> Reslets dans l'Eau
> Ongles
> Gruyère
> Le parfum qui fut
> Le ventre dans la plaine
>   by Debussy
>   Encore: Corsage

Only one person would have written that, I thought as I sprang up, turned around and there she was a few tables away, twinkling at me. Devoted to her own race, she loved to tell Jewish stories with a nice Whitechapel accent. When it became necessary to assert herself against two of her managers who had almost the same Christian name she said 'When I have to expostulate with Mary A. I say 'Now, now, Mary' (putting on her most persuasive tone) 'but with Mary B. I *scream!*' She loved games, bridge and canasta and solitaire,[1] which she frequently played by way of relaxation in the afternoon before a recital. She was adept at anagrams and we sometimes exchanged them at the ends of letters—'I did one of the anagrams in the berth—about 2 A.M.' Occasionally she referred to herself as 'Hyra Mess'. And at those delightful parties after the concerts when she was relaxed and serene in the thought that things had gone reasonably well (she was never completely satisfied) she would sometimes add to the hilarity of the company by playing the Chopin Black Key Study with an orange, the Scarlatti Sonata in C major with two carrots, or sing Nevin's *Rosary* à la Bloomsbury lodging-house landlady in a thick contralto just a shade flat. Or if the occasion seemed more serious she would introduce her hearers to the recently-written Frank Bridge Sonata, though she had already played a full-length programme. She was quite

---

[1] Solitaire (Amer.) = Patience (Eng.). (Ed.)

disappointed when New York failed to approve of the Bridge: and this lack of enthusiasm may have convinced her that her audience did not demand that she play modern music, toward which she herself had reservations. One day she asked me to play Hindemith's *Ludus tonalis* for her, but I think she did not really like it.

While in her earlier years she would include Debussy, Ravel, Bax, O'Donnell's *Before the Dawn* and even for American audiences *The White Peacock* of Griffes, these items were gradually eliminated from her repertoire and she concentrated on her real favourites, the German composers; she preferred substantial food to 'grieps of little pouces', but she eschewed the grandiose; she dared to begin one of her earliest New York recitals with four preludes and fugues from the *Well-Tempered Clavier* instead of a transcription from the organ works. Her own transcriptions were of quiet compositions. She was one of the first pianists to play the Schubert sonatas in America where they had been considered diffuse. The first one she presented was the A major Op. 120 and she was quite nervous about it, as she told Mr. Matthay when she took it to him for a special lesson. Her managers were told to impress on prospective audiences that it was 'light and short'. In her later years, encouraged by the enthusiastic reception of this sonata as well as the A minor Op. 143 and the B flat, she resurrected three of the comparatively unknown Klavierstücke. Chopin disappeared from her recitals, Liszt she never played and Franck lost his charm for her. On the other hand her devotion to Mozart increased and she took great delight in playing his concertos, notably the G major and the early E flat. With characteristic modesty she approached the last Beethoven sonatas with caution, but once she had convinced herself that she could play them, the three final sonatas took first place in her mind. The last recital I heard her give and the last but one in America consisted of these sonatas alone. After Op. 111 she would refuse to play an encore, 'What can you play after that?' she would say, addressing the audience.

This ability to take her hearers into her confidence, to speak to them, was another indication of the development of her character, for as a girl she had been too shy, as she confessed, to make a speech; but particularly after the war this reserve was surmounted with the happiest results. She no longer feared to say engagingly to the assemblage in explanation of playing with music, 'I do really know my music, but I know you want me to be comfortable.' As a matter of fact her memory was remarkably secure. In her very earliest years, she admitted, she had once forgotten an entrance in the Mozart D minor Concerto and had been obliged to come in 'on all fours'. The very tricky last movement of the Schumann Concerto which Donald Tovey said he had never played without making a slip, always in a different place, held no terrors for her and she played it from memory even in the latter years. Once I remarked, 'Myra, you use your spectacles when you practise from notes, can you *really* see the music without them? I can't,' and she replied slyly 'I can *just* see it.' When she played the Mozart concertos she used the full orchestral scores. As everyone knows, the practice of playing from memory grew up only a little over a century ago (Clara Schumann is said to have wept over the 'necessity' of doing it) and Myra Hess felt that at least in America far too much stress was laid on memorizing to the endangering of a near-perfect performance; many who have taught students will agree, having found that as soon as they concentrate on memorizing their feeling for the music evaporates in the face of their anxiety over the exact notes.

She subjugated conductors as well as audiences. After Koussewitsky, always difficult with artists, had made her first rehearsal with him thoroughly disagreeable, he reversed his tactics; and when I asked her what had changed his attitude she replied with characteristic modesty 'I think it was the music.' After that somewhat inauspicious beginning he had her appear with the Boston Symphony each year; and after he had retired and she was never asked to

play with it again, to the stupefaction and fury of her devoted Boston audience, all she would say in response to in-
quiries was 'I suppose it is a case of "Vive la France".'

Koussewitsky became her devoted friend as did many
other American musicians like Harold Bauer; but she also
attracted those who were distinguished in other arts, like
Willa Cather, Ruth Draper and Thornton Wilder. It was of
course natural that the Steinways should become her lifelong
and grateful admirers and she was almost in the position of a
daughter to the elder Mrs. Steinway whose death she felt
most keenly. To other young and old artists she was generous and sympathetic; but she could be delightfully 'catty'
concerning those who showed obvious egotism, for that she
could not endure. I once expressed my admiration of her
extraordinarily perfect performance of the difficult last
movement of Bach's *Italian Concerto* and she immediately
responded 'You know I have played that movement for
years, and I don't think it has ever "gone" until today.'

Since I never studied with Myra Hess I cannot speak
authoritatively of her teaching. But I can imagine what
she demanded of her pupils: the acquisition of a beautiful
tone; an unremitting attention to the meaning and form
of the phrase; an unbroken legato when legato was appropriate (with no concealment of a faulty legato by using the
damper pedal); vital rhythm; a dramatic projection of the
sense. I do not suppose that she prescribed endless études
to promote brilliancy. She herself was not interested in playing flashy music (she said to Yolanda Mero 'I like to hear
you play Liszt, but I cannot play it') and her own playing
was not primarily outstanding in virtuosity. I once asked
an elderly lady who had heard Clara Schumann how the
two pianists differed. Devoted to Myra's playing, she replied, 'Oh, Clara was much more brilliant.' Like many of
her race, Myra's hand was small; she could not reach a
tenth, and sometimes the large chords were a little smashed.
But the hand was muscular and there was nothing puny
about her playing.

The genesis of her transcription 'Jesu, Joy of Man's Desiring' which became so popular and was imitated by other transcribers, Harold Bauer among them, was, she told me, that she had heard a chorus at Oxford singing the original from Bach's cantata *Herz und Mund und That und Leben* and was struck with its beauty which at that time was almost unknown. The way she set it down on paper is significant of her attention to line, for instead of writing chords she went out of her way to give different stems to notes in different lines. The result looks complicated but it was the best way to show the counterpoint.

She considered that she owed everything to the teaching of Matthay, to whom she went when she was thirteen. As a matter of fact she had at that time much to learn. It should be encouraging to students to realize that her infectious rhythm was not achieved without years of work to bring her latent sense of it to the fore. In those days it was not completely reliable. 'There was some scrimmaging and bolting,' Mrs. Matthay remarked of an early performance of the Haydn Variations. Myra Hess herself complained that she was a very slow worker; how really slow she was it is impossible to say, but the standard of perfection she demanded of herself could never have been attained quickly; and she was probably always comparing herself with her great friend and co-pupil Irene Scharrer, who was gifted with an unusual natural fluency. Her will-power was extraordinary. Once I heard her singing (in an almost bass voice) as she played, and I told her so. 'Am I *singing*?' She inquired. 'I'll stop that.' I never heard her sing again.

What moments of special beauty do I remember from the many but still too-infrequent times when I heard her? The perfection of her scales at the beginning of the Beethoven C minor Concerto; the sparkle of the Gigue from the Bach 5th French Suite; the irresistible gaiety of the Scarlatti Sonata in G; the serene delivery of the opening theme of the Schubert B flat Sonata; the exquisite tone of the slow movement of the F minor Brahms Sonata; the intoxicating

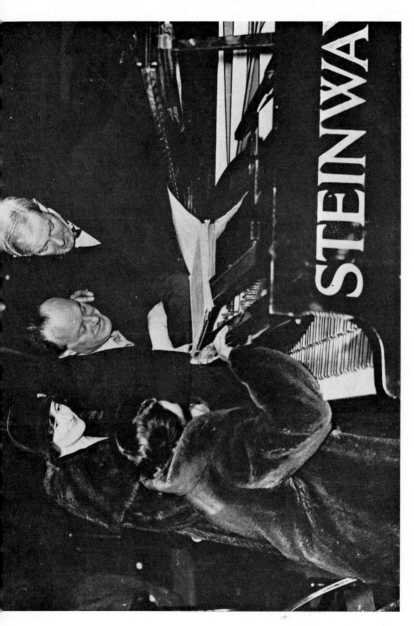

MYRA WITH IRENE SCHARRER, HAROLD SAMUEL AND SIR HAMILTON HARTY, IN THE 1930'S

MYRA WITH DENISE LASSIMONNE IN ITALY, 1937

rhythm of the last movement of Mozart's G major Concerto;
the whispered answer to the orchestra in the second movement of Beethoven's G major Concerto; the lilt of the
Brahms Intermezzo in C. Her musical colleagues recognized
her special aptitudes and abilities when a dozen of them
gathered together in New York to play Schumann's *Carnaval*, uniting (horrible thought) in the Preambule and
Davidsbündler March. Solos were assigned to each and Myra
Hess was selected to play Eusebius.

No one in America was surprised when at the outbreak
of the war she cancelled all plans for another tour and
elected to stay in England, exposing herself to indescribable
dangers. But even those who had known her best were impressed by the talent for organization which she showed in
creating the National Gallery Concerts. I will leave to others
the account of these, only remarking on passing that never
could we have imagined Myra Hess making a speech in
Trafalgar Square![1] Her courage at that time can be judged
from a letter dated 2nd December, 1940, in which she
wrote:

'Life is so incredible that even the seasons seem unreal.
The rest of my life has been a "holiday" and after a
strenuous day one's mind seems to be blank, perhaps mer-
cifully so . . I must explain at once that my own home
is safe and sound (always touching wood . . .) but it is
too inaccessible in these "unusually" difficult winter
months. It seemed like the hand of the Lord when the
lady next door to A. and her sister fled from London and
wanted to let her house . . . I have taken it by the month
(for a mere song . . . or perhaps a cadenza . . .) and when
M. and A. are not on night duty we can spend the long
evenings together with music and bridge . . . (with re-
percussive slams without!) . . .

'We never have a shade of doubt about the ultimate
triumph of Light over Darkness. I only hope we shall

---

[1] See p. 94 of 'The National Gallery Concerts and After'. (Ed.)

keep our sanity when we turn on all the lights and open curtains wide . . .

'Although there have been various vicissitudes . . . we have not missed a day's concert at the National Gallery . . . These last weeks have been particularly strenuous, and my programmes so varied that I sometimes feel like the chameleon who burst when placed upon a piece of Scotch plaid . . . I play almost every single week at the N.G. and have been giving recitals in the Provinces, to say nothing of the tremendous task of planning five programmes a week ad infinitum . . .

'You ask me if I practise? Precious little . . . at least *the kind of practising I like to do*'(italics mine) 'but the Lord seems to be with me and when music is needed as never before the imagination seems to be forthcoming when one actually gets to the concert.

'For months and even now at times it is almost impossible to sit down in cold blood and practise "passages and notes". . .

'It is incredible how we can adapt ourselves to a state of existence beyond the direst imagination, but the steady belief that "all will be well" keeps us sane and full of determination.'

Some idea of the nervous strain of those days is revealed in the story she told of playing the Beethoven C minor Concerto in Albert Hall during the worst of the buzz-bomb attacks. During the long introduction one was heard approaching; as it came nearer and nearer, her ear (as she put it) 'stretched higher and higher' in momentary expectation of the cut-out. The moment for her first entrance arrived; she 'came in' on the dot, an octave too high!

When she returned to America it was as a national heroine of Britain, and when she was created Dame of the British Empire, the news was received in the United States with as much satisfaction as if she had been partly American.

The success of Myra Hess in America had considerable

effect on the reputation of Matthay there where his work before her New York debut had been almost unknown. One of the first things asked when a new pianist makes a spectacular success is the name of his teacher. So it is not surprising that after 1922 Matthay was sought out by an increasing number of American students, particularly in the summer, and that he began to have what might almost have been called an American summer school. He was the first person to recognize her influence in bringing about this situation. It may be said that the considerable number of Americans today who teach with reference to his principles would not have been as large as it is if it had not been for Myra Hess. Certainly his books, excellent as they are, would not have made the impact on the public that was made by her playing. A similar situation had arisen at the end of the nineteenth century when Paderewski's success sent many Americans to his teacher Leschetizsky. But few teachers have been fortunate enough to be represented by a pupil who in her own right was such an outstanding personality. Myra Hess was much more than a skilled exponent of Matthay's ideas. While she proved their validity up to the hilt and demonstrated how musical teaching can release latent powers of expression, she herself was a person of ripe understanding, imaginative, passionate, compassionate temperament, sensitive to the tragedy of life and to its joy.

She was a truly noble woman.

Music in Place of Pictures

BY

SIR KENNETH CLARK

SOON AFTER war was declared the air-raid siren sounded and we all took our gas masks and went to our shelters. We were slightly nervous, but cheerful and excited, like nuns in a new convent. It turned out to be a false alarm, but it was typical of the unreal anxieties of those first weeks. Partly from a reasonable prudence, partly from a feeling that something must be done to show that we were taking the war seriously, and partly in a spirit of contrition, the Home Office had decided to close down anything that could cheer and console us. No theatres, no concerts, no picture galleries. Even the art dealers were closed. For the first two or three nights the black-out was beautiful and poetic. Thereafter it combined with a lack of entertainment to make people irritable. It became the symbol of their frustration. People spoke of a 'cultural black-out'.

Of all the institutions thus turned from a positive to a negative function, the National Gallery presented the dreariest spectacle. Every picture had been taken away, but the frames remained, and multiplied the general emptiness with a series of smaller emptinesses. When I returned to the Gallery, after the first all-absorbing task of evacuation was more or less safely over, I walked round those large, dirty, and (as it turned out) ill-proportioned rooms, in deep depression.

Into this atmosphere of defeat and gloom came the conquering, radiant presence of Myra Hess. I do not keep a diary, or records of any sort, but I think she was accompanied by Miss Denise Lassimonne. I am sure that what she proposed was to give an occasional concert in the Gallery, to which I (not knowing the difficulties involved) said 'Why not give one every day?' This had already been in her mind but she had been too bashful of authority to suggest it. In a few minutes everything was agreed; that at least was an advantage of the war, that one felt no need to ask permission of Trustees or Treasury, although at a later stage this seems to have been done. While Myra began composing programmes the rest of us looked for chairs and a platform and draped the Board Room curtains over one side of the octagon in a hopeless attempt to give the Gallery a vestige of baroque splendour. An old photograph reminds me that we even managed to find some pictures that we had not thought worth evacuating.

I do not think that anyone who was present at the first concert will forget it. It was given by Myra 'In case', she said, 'the whole thing should be a failure.' The main work was Beethoven's Appassionata, and at the end she played that piece which always seemed so personal to her, a piano rendering of 'Jesu, Joy of Man's Desiring'. I stood behind one of the curtains, and looked at the packed audience. They had come with anxious, hungry faces, but as they listened to the music and looked at Myra's rapt expression, they lost the thought of their private worries. I had never seen faces so transformed, and said to myself 'This is how men and women must have looked at the great preachers who gave them back their courage and faith.' What made those early concerts more than musical performances was Myra's sublime optimism. I do not mean optimism about the outcome of the war, on which subject she probably felt as doubtful as any other reasonable person. I am thinking of her belief that a majority of human beings could share the emotions of love, pity, brotherhood and resignation that the great composers have expressed in their music. She was herself an entirely affirmative character and for this reason was able to express the feeling of simple, unified enthusiasm that marks the beginning of a national crisis. Doubt and disillusion were foreign to her nature, and the present questioning

of all decent standards must have been incomprehensible
to her.

Although she had high standards of technical skill for
herself, as for everyone else, she believed that the music
was more important than the performance: or, at least, she
had no neurotic feelings about perfection. She gave out with
inexhaustible generosity and, if the audience was responsive,
would cheerfully go on playing all day. When I spoke of
the strain of giving so many performances at the Gallery,
she replied that she had to practise for so many hours a day
anyway, and might as well do so for people who were enjoying it. She belonged to a generation of musicians who were
not too far removed from the music-halls: warm-hearted,
uncomplicated, unself-pitying. She insisted that the first
orchestral concert we put on at the Gallery should be conducted by Sir Henry Wood. In the National Gallery her
love of a good popular entertainment only once got the
better of her, on New Year's Day, 1940, when nine well-
known pianists, playing musical chairs, took turns at
Schumann's *Carnaval*; and the Toy Symphony was performed under my baton, with admirable precision on the
part of the quail (Elena Gerhardt) but regrettable frivolity
on the part of the cuckoos (Irene Scharrer and Myra Hess).

However, I must quickly correct any false impression
which the last paragraph may have produced. It is true
that Myra had a certain Browningesque heartiness, which
showed itself particularly when she was playing Beethoven
or Brahms. But the earnestness and sincerity of her character suggested deep resources; and it was this feeling of depth,
of unvarying quality—which inspired all of us who worked
with her in her 'great adventure'.

Julia M.

BY

JOYCE GRENFELL

THIS IS a sketch of Myra rather than a portrait. Ours was an easy relationship lasting many years and, after periodic separations when either of us was abroad, we picked up at exactly the point we had left off. I don't think one can really know anyone completely unless one has been through thick and thin together, and until her last illness I had never been with Myra in adversity; so although she was very open and talked freely to me I always sensed a final privacy in her and I think our relationship was close rather than intimate.

She was named Julia Myra and when we first met she told me she had never liked the name Myra and wished she had been called Julia. I always wrote to her as Julia M. and that is the way she signed her letters to me.

In her last tour of the United States her press notices were probably the best she ever had in a lifetime of good notices. One in particular summed up what her playing meant to so many of her vast audiences, and to me. In effect the writer said that he did not go to a Myra Hess concert to hear Myra Hess, he went to hear music.

This was her special magic.

There she sat, adjusting the piano stool until she was entirely comfortable, taking her time about it; wiped her palms on the inevitable handkerchief, lifted those small remarkable hands, and then devoted herself to producing music.

Because she had greatness, and stature, it isn't always easy to remember that she was in fact a small woman. She was dark and pleasingly plump with very bright dark eyes, and she always wore her hair parted in the middle and arranged in two shallow scallops on her forehead and drawn back into a bun at the back. She had small feet on fine-boned ankles and walked with a slight spring, shifting her weight from foot to foot like a sailor. It was a young walk and lasted until her illness. Her shoulders rose when she laughed, and this was agreeably often, and when she was deeply amused she not only shook but bowed from the waist. Her voice was low and gentle and within her inner circle of friends she spoke a sort of private language that might read a bit 'fancy' if quoted but, spoken, it had her own individual flavour.

She wrote a beautiful hand, firm and clear. It lay on the page like a drawing and seemed to move with rhythm, going slightly uphill from left to right. She used a pen with a broad flexible nib and her strokes were bold and generous, no flourishes but a stylish grace. At one time she wrote on very thick blue paper in black ink.

I first knew her in the Wildwood Road days. We met staying with Mrs. Holland Martin at Overbury, under Bredon Hill, for a Three Choirs Festival in 1937. It was a large house-party, half musicians taking part in the Festival and the rest Festival followers. As I remember, Walford Davies, Astra Desmond, Elsie Suddaby, Keith Falkner and Myra were there, and the sun shone every day of that lovely September. Or so it now seems. There was tennis on grass courts, delicious foods eaten at an enormous table, and the atmosphere was congenial. Every morning sparkling dew lay on the long lawn towards the Vale of Gloucester bordered by beds planted only with blue or white flowers.

One late afternoon the talk turned to the subject of gaiety in music. To illustrate a point Walford got up and went to the piano to play a minuet from a little known opera by Handel. Then Myra took over and played the G major Gigue of Bach. It is dance music and was not to be resisted at that moment. Walford, then in his seventies I think, led me into an unpremeditated jig that took us in and out of the chairs and tables all round the room. The jig then turned into a Grand Chain and everyone else joined in. Myra, carried away too, was bouncing on her piano stool. I have an idea that we also sang as we wove our way out of the drawing-room and into the hall, half way up the broad staircase and down again, until we finally fell gasping into sofas and chairs. When he could speak Walford said he thought Bach might have liked it.

This happened a very long time ago, but I remember it vividly as one of the most enjoyable moments of spontaneous exuberance I have ever experienced. It isn't often that the British let go but when they do it is startling enough to make an indelible mark.

I was one of the fortunate people who worked in Irene Gater's Canteen run for Myra's National Gallery Concerts in the war. We made sandwiches that became justly famous for being complementary to the music. They were delicious. Special favourites were honey and raisin in fresh brown bread; cream cheese and date; ham and chutney; and there were generous slices of good damp station cake, as well as strong coffee. I often had the job of carrying a tray of these refreshments to the artists room before the concerts.

Myra came to the Gallery almost every day, usually with her niece Beryl Davis, who was acting as her secretary at that time while Anita (Saz) Gunn, her peace time secretary, was a driver in the Ambulance Service. I used to sit with Myra and Beryl in a big empty gallery behind the platform, out of sight of the audience. This was a luxurious way to hear music; privately and in a large undisturbing space. It was also an education, and it was there that I learned to prefer chamber music to all other kinds.

Those wartime concerts were much more than a comfort and a refreshment. I think the music was a reminder of the continuity, unaltered in spite of the horrors, of something real and durable. It made one realise that eternity is not miles of nothing going on for ever and ever, but is the recognition of spiritual values, unchanging and eternally here, now. I think it was this awareness of something permanent in a world where everything seemed to be collapsing and evaporating that restored a sense of balance and lifted our hearts.

Perhaps in the conventional sense Myra was not religious but her awareness of the spirit was very real. We had many conversations about this, and about faith and belief. I think she had a thirst for faith and did not seem able completely to assuage it. Although she knew she was greatly gifted, and accepted the fact with simple grace, her humility was genuine. There was an innocence about her that remained natural all her life: it was as if she looked on wonder with the eyes of a child. She knew her playing had a profound effect on audiences and this moved her as her playing moved them, but she found it hard to believe she had ever done really well.

I think she never played at a concert without going through agonies of apprehension. Some of this is probably necessary for an artist. It is not the same thing as 'nerves'. It is a limbering up and calling in of forces that brings concentration into a fine, working instrument of precision. I believe 'nerves' come from uncertainty of preparation and are partly a kind of guilt: this can be very destructive. Apprehension is useful, for it exercises a final control. Myra's tension before a performance seemed to be essential to her but she never got used to it and it was painful.

Myra had an element of actress in her. Saz remembers her frowning with concentration and apprehension in the artists room, scowling even to the very edge of the platform, but there, just before she went on, she would put on a concert face, designed to inspire confidence. She explained she had to *look* as if she was enjoying herself or nobody else would.

Recording and broadcasting were, of course, part of her life, but she once told me she felt it was almost impossible to play as one wanted to, and knew one could, once the red light was on in the studio. Psychologically this signal, that

means *now* one is being recorded or is on the air, can have
a restricting and even crippling effect. It is an on-the-spot
judgement, with taped evidence to prove its terrible vigil-
ance. Myra said its worst effect was that it prevented one
from taking risks and taking risks is what gives a performance vitality and individuality. I think she disliked her
own recordings because, except in the case of recorded public
concerts when she was able to forget that little red light,
she never felt free to take the risks she wanted to.

We speak in clichés of performances being inspired and
inspiring and of enlightened experiences. But a cliché is
a cliché simply because it is true enough to have lasted.
It is almost impossible to write about Myra's playing without drawing on clichés, so I must write that her playing was
often both inspired and inspiring. The feeling I had about
it was a new-every-morning freshness. She could play a
long familiar work as if it was for the very first time and
display it for us as, surely, it must have first occurred to the
composer.

I crossed the Atlantic with Myra several times. Except
for the war she played in America every year, usually going
over there in January and coming home again in April. The
Cunard Line arranged for a cottage piano to be moved into
her stateroom and there she spent the whole trip, seldom
going out at all. The sea journey was a precious time of
privacy and near-isolation, rare and therefore useful to her
for refreshment before the demanding tour that lay ahead.
She had all her meals sent to the stateroom and often spent
the day in a dressing-gown with her hair down, tied back
with a ribbon like a schoolgirl's. She always obeyed a wise
instinct for self preservation in order to reserve her energies
for the essential job. At home a hairdresser came to her:
so did the dressmaker, or else she had dresses sent to her
on approval to try on in her own room. In the twenty-nine
years that I knew her I could count her visits to my house
on the fingers of one hand, but she invited me to come and
see her times beyond counting. We also talked frequently

on the telephone. On board ship she looked forward to *not* talking on the telephone or writing letters. Instead she read novels and played games.

For she was a games addict. Bridge, canasta, back-gammon, scrabble, and above all patience were her pleasure. She knew every kind of patience and this was one of her solaces when she could no longer play the piano. Until this time of illness she never missed doing the crossword puzzle in *The Times* and usually finished it before lunch.

Saz Gunn told me she thought Myras games of patience fulfilled a demand, always strong in her, for resolution: the solving of a problem. The unattainable horizon of music was never arrived at. Myra loved tidy conclusions, the drawn line at the end of the sum. When all her cards came out in patience it was like drawing a final line. She often played a game before a concert and when it came out she felt a freedom. Perhaps another reason why patience was so important to her in the last years when she could no longer play the piano, was because it gave her a way of using her hands.

On board ship she and Saz Gunn played endless games of cards, and sometimes when it was scrabble I played too. (I can't tell a club from a spade without a lot of considera-tion, so cards are not for me.) They were experts and knew every permitted two-letter word in the dictionary and even allowed such illegalities as Ra, the Sun God, a proper noun, and pi a symbol in mathematics, but o.k. and po were out. Myra played scrabble with the malice aforethought of a Russian chess champion and was very hard to beat. She even hissed a little in a villainous way as she planned her next relentless move.

One year I too was going to work in America and the purser arranged for me to borrow a small games room with a piano in it somewhere well out of earshot, high among the chimney stacks on the top deck. Myra said why shouldn't she play my songs for me to rehearse, so one evening I took the music to her stateroom. Richard Addinsell had set a group of pastiche encores for my programme. There was a noble Elgarian one, a French Bergerette and others; but the one Myra liked playing best was a florid vehicle for a showy mezzo-sop' who is reluctant to stop. 'And now my song is ended, I'll sing for thee no more', she promises, falsely as it turns out. It has a splendidly pretentious introduction of cascading octaves and passionate chords and we had a good time doing it, encoring ourselves several times over and adding quality, so we thought, with every rendering.

Whenever I had written a new lyric or a monologue I always took it to show to Myra. She listened like a child does, giving herself to the story and was a responsive audience, attentive and generous.

In New York she stayed at the Laurelton Hotel, a small old-fashioned place that was, for New York, moderately quiet. Her rooms faced the back of Carnegie Hall a block away and in the studios above the auditorium you could see ballet dancing classes going on and sometimes an ardent singer with his mouth open singing unheard across the merciful distance. Myra introduced me to the Laurelton and I stayed there whenever I was in New York. Steinway's, like the Cunard Line, had a piano waiting for her at the hotel, and you could hardly see the room for flowers, not only on the day she arrived but throughout her stay. She was never without flowers wherever she went. They arrived before and after concerts and in between times. Many were home grown and arrived lovingly bunched and wrapped in damp tissue paper from country friends and followers. There were also more formal bouquets, and the long room in Cavendish Close, where she lived for the last thirteen years of her life, always had at least one big bowl of flowers in the far window and smaller bunches on the piano and mantelpiece.

At the Laurelton she was soon settled in. Her special stiff-leaved month-at-a-glance diary lay open on the desk, already full of engagements. Beside it was a box of her

favourite soft black Eberhard Faber pencils with their cunn-
ingly fitted erasers that can be adjusted to pull out further
and produce more and more rubber. Anita Gunn was established in a nearby room where the telephone rang con-
tinuously and the welcome to America, where Myra was
loved more warmly even than at home, had begun and
went on throughout her stay.

All the hotel staff knew her and were devoted. Gaston,
who runs the newspaper stand in the Wellington Hotel next
door, was a special friend. When she became a Dame there
was slight confusion at first, for 'dame', as it is used in
America, they found difficult to equate with someone so
respected. All was understood when they learned it was an
honourable address.

I once went to a morning rehearsal for an orchestral concert Myra was playing in later that evening at Carnegie
Hall. Except for the National Gallery Concerts I don't think
I had ever before been with her before a big concert, so
it was a surprise to me to see how far she removed herself,
as it were, so long before the performance. We met in the
lobby of the hotel to walk a block up Seventh Avenue to
Carnegie. She smiled from a long way off and instinct told
me not to speak and we walked in silence. Already she had
moved into a place where she could not be approached. If
this sounds in any way affected or pretentious I have failed
in my account of it. It was natural and right for her and
one never questioned it. By the time she had taken off her
coat and greeted the conductor she had returned from her
place of preparation, acknowledged the smiling welcome
from the standing orchestra, and was again in full communication.

Myra was interested in people and they responded. Unlike some artists she was not self-absorbed although, as I
have said, she knew how to preserve her energies and was
disciplined about keeping spaces for rest and preparation.
But she also gave much spare time to her friends and probably had more life-stories and aspirations poured into her

ear than anyone I know. But, in turn, she was an essentially private person, and I always felt she kept what seemed to be an essential, if small, barrier between herself and even her close friends in spite of a genuine wish for inclusion. Perhaps all great artists have this final isolation.

She was a centre for affection and I think everyone who came in touch with her felt some sense of privilege, for she was a person apart, endowed with that extra measure of magic allowed to unusually gifted people. It wasn't her fame or her music alone that drew them. I think it was her affinity with something we sensed she had discovered that we needed to know. She was quite unaware of this and would, I think, have denied any such discovery. She had a sixth sense for genuine and undemanding appreciation but I believe she was uncomfortable with hero-worship. All stars attract by their light, and hers shone brightly. She was, in my view, rightly impersonal on the platform. That is why the music came to us so clearly; she never got between it and the hearer. Off the platform she was a warm and individual woman and the public sensed this, and she had to be protected from the followers and fans or they might have swallowed her up.

Mr. Worman of Ibbs and Tillett, who for many years stage-managed so many of her concerts, kept a firm hand on the door of the artists room after a performance. Crowds rushed there to pay homage and they had to be controlled. It was interesting to mark the differences in their approach. There were simple appreciators who came to say thank you and moved on after shaking her hand. Some wanted to identify themselves with her and stood long explaining why they alone were able to understand, demanding as of a right her attention and time. These were sometimes sad figures, refugees perhaps, hungry for acknowledgement in a new country. Often they were just egotists fighting to prove by their contact with Myra that they really rated. Some were plain bores, but most were ordinary listeners who had had a good time and wanted to tell her so.

Mr. Worman, one of her most devoted admirers, was a controlled man used to concerts and artists, but he was often visibly moved by Myra's playing and would shake his head in wonder as if to say 'I don't know how she does it'.

Nor, I'm sure, did she. That was part of her power.

There are so many anecdotes about her usually told by Myra against herself. One was about a war-time recital she gave in a much bombed town in the South of England. It was a civic affair arranged to boost morale and show that Britons could take it. As she was about to go on to the platform, led by the Mayor who was to introduce her, he turned to her and said: 'Oh—I forgot to ask—what instrument is it you play?'

There is, alas, no foundation for my favourite Myra story but to this day I like to pretend it was true. Legend tells that she and Irene Scharrer, who were life-long friends, were sitting in the front row at a meeting of the Musicians' Benevolent Fund. They were not paying attention to what was being said on the platform, and coming-to at the end of some pronouncement unanimously felt it was a moment needing a reaction of some sort, and so they, alone and in unison, clapped their hands loudly together. It seems that the pronouncement had been about some ghastly disaster and the one thing it hadn't called for was enthusiastic applause. Ever after and to this day many of her friends and I receive an item of bad news with a clap. This is open to misinterpretation, but I think it is a useful comment on a lot of bad news, although time, place and sensibility have to dictate its suitability.

Myra held that this story really originated in a revue sketch that Beatrice Lillie appeared in. For me it remains the sole property of Myra and Irene.

She was sympathetic and helpful to refugee musicians who came to England from Germany. One soloist had a name that in English sounded decidedly rude. It was not easy to explain this to him for he had almost no English, or humour, but she did so with tact and wondered if per-

Photo: Ronald Proctor

MYRA WITH BERYL DAVIS, 1941

Photo : Ronald Proctor

MYRA TALKING TO THE AUDIENCE AT A NATIONAL GALLERY CONCERT

haps he would consider changing his name for British audiences? He took her advice and acted upon it but on the professional cards he had printed there appeared, in brackets under the new cleaned up version, his old rude name.

The only known concession Myra ever made to Hitler was involuntary. She was playing the C minor Concerto of Beethoven at the Albert Hall when a V.2 bomb exploded somewhere well within earshot. Startled, Myra's hands rose from the keys and came down again an octave higher than Beethoven had suggested. It took skill and ingenuity to climb down again to the right place. She made it satisfactorily.

Myra's party turns were unfailingly enjoyable. She made a life-like Queen Victoria under a lace doily, and her rolled orange performance of the black-note Study of Chopin was a triumph of skill and ingenuity. I think my favourite was her imitation of a mechanical piano, correct and deadly.

In the game of Analogies I would list Myra like this:

Colour: Apricot.
Furniture: Comfortable leather dining-room chair, easy but supporting.
Fruit: Apricot (again), tangy, sweet, firm.
Animal: Pony, lively but reliable.
Flower: Zinnia

This is a very personal view. Generally she was recognised as a great artist, true, instinctive and unselfconscious. Rarest of all perhaps, she was what she appeared to be; a dear, courteous woman of charm and complete humility.

Soon it will be possible to forget the last sad years, for they are short compared to a long life of interest and achievement. It was a difficult period for her, for just as she used to withdraw into herself before a performance so she seemed to withdraw at this hard time. It was as if she could not find the weapons she needed to fight the situation, and she found little consolation or philosophical comfort in looking back at the years of happiness and success. There was no bitterness, only a sad perplexity.

Already I see her again as she was, smiling and walking forward in that springing way she had; and I remember her bawdy sense of humour and her infectious laugh. Lately it was the absence of this quick response that was so distressing to her friends, for it was unfamiliar; but the last time I saw her, a few weeks before she died, I told her a simple story of earthy vulgarity and it touched some remaining chord in her and she was instantly swept into a gust of immediate delight. Her shoulders rose and shook and she bowed from the waist in the old way and she said: 'Oh no!' with a little moan of pleasure,'Oh *no*!'

So I am able to remember her as she once was and undoubtedly is, free of strain and burdens, spontaneous and serene.

For thousands of people she turned a key and opened a door into a new dimension of music. I am grateful to be one of their number, and to count her as a dear friend.

Myra on Holiday

BY

FRANK MANNHEIMER

MYRA BROUGHT to her holidays all the gusto and enthusiasm which were such a vital part of her music
making. Whether the holiday was planned for rest,
a journey abroad to see new places, a single day taken out
of a busy tour, or just going to the theatre, Myra would
give the aura of a special event to the occasion. There were
often rapid changes of mood from abandoned gaiety to wist-
fulness, from being completely carefree to feeling sudden
bouts of deep concern, and there would often be long
interruptions in card games for serious discussions of music.
There was always the feeling of increased enjoyment because time was being taken from serious work. A holiday
was a stolen pleasure like that a child gets from playing truant
from school. Myra used to sing a little song for us which
she had sung as a small child in a children's play. I cannot
recall the entire text, but the last line of the song was
' . . . and my name is little Tootsie Wee.' And so the nick-
name of 'Tootsie' was adopted, and it was as the carefree
singer of that little song that Myra would embark on holidays.

We were staying in the house of friends in Dorset, one
spring before the war, and had gone for a walk through the
countryside. We discovered a lovely little church and found
the vicar delighted to show us around. Later he told us of
a path through open fields, a far more attractive route than
the one we had taken. He led us to the stile we must cross
to find the footpath through the fields and after saying our
farewells we started off. Myra crossed the stile first, slipped
as she got over and fell rolling in the grass. I jumped quickly

on to the stile but before I could get down she sat up, laughing uproariously, and said 'What exquisite grace.' 'A beautiful performance,' I said, applauding heartily. It was only when we heard the voice of our vicar-guide making mild comments of disapproval that we realized he had witnessed this scene. I jumped down hastily, helped Myra up, and like naughty children we said an embarrassed 'Good afternoon' and started along our path. 'I feel just as though I were back in the nursery' was Myra's comment as we began our walk through the fields. We collected a few wild-flowers and quite suddenly Myra was thinking aloud about the next season's programmes and exploring all sorts of combinations of works. When we got back to the house where we were staying, she gave a hilarious account of our afternoon's adventure and she did not revert to talk about the programmes all the time we were in Dorset.

Myra's close friends knew of her intense love of games, and on all holidays, playing cards or 'Scrabble' punctuated the day's activities. When her mood would alter, the game might be temporarily suspended. We spent a holiday on Lake Maggiore, staying in the house of another friend. We were sitting on the terrace which overlooks the lake and the Alps beyond, playing the usual game of cards when suddenly Myra began speaking of a pianist friend who had been forced to discontinue public playing because of a physical handicap. We stopped our game and walked along the terrace as Myra spoke of her deep concern for her friend's future. Without a word she went in to the drawing room, and sat down at the piano and played the slow movement of the posthumous B flat major Sonata by Schubert more beautifully than I shall ever hear it again. When she finished she seemed unaware that tears were streaming down her face. Silently she got up from the piano and went out on to the terrace again.

Anything which gave the feeling of change or relaxation of accustomed routine was welcomed by Myra and she particularly enjoyed an improvised picnic. We had many of these; on the Suffolk coast near Aldeburgh, in the mountains on the Swiss-Italian border, sitting in a car munching sandwiches late at night on our way back to London after attending a performance at the Three Choirs Festival and in the California countryside on the day following one of her most memorable performances of the Beethoven G major Concerto. That evening the audience was so deeply moved by her playing that it rose as one man and, ceasing to applaud, stood in near-silence as she reappeared on the stage. The next day we motored into the country and after lunching under the trees she stretched out in a deck chair alternately talking and dozing off. The following morning she was back at the piano ready to resume her tour.

After the death of Mrs. Matthay we always spent Christmas holidays with our adored teacher, Tobias Matthay, at his house in Surrey. Myra and I would usually sit up very late over a final game of cards. When the 'final' game was over, Myra would say 'Of course it is madness to sit up so late but we aren't too tired for one more game, are we?' Those post-midnight games were always interrupted by long conversations. We knew that Mr. Matthay (or 'Punkey' as we affectionately nicknamed him) was sleeping in the room just above us and we avoided the usual outbursts of laughter. In the early hours of one morning, the door suddenly opened and Punkey entered the room wearing his long dressing gown and the inevitable little velvet skull cap. It was like a pantomime performance. He came in to the room, placed two glasses, a bottle of whisky and a syphon of soda on the table, walked to the door, turned, bowed formally and left the room without uttering a word. We both burst out laughing and the door opened again as he gave an encore bow before he returned to his room, still without a word. Myra with the sudden change of mood to which I was so accustomed said simply, 'What a saint he is and how lucky we are'.

The last holiday we had together was in Sicily. The brief diary Myra kept of that holiday records visits to Greek theatres and ruins, to museums and churches, and frequently there is a reference to 'games' and, recalling some special pleasure or surprise, to 'parties'. She also records amusing incidents such as . . . 'April 23 . . . Shampoo . . . quickest on record. Chappie born in New York, so spoke English (quite good too). I apologized for my old fashioned head. He replied "Hair; and, if I may say so, reminds me of pictures of Queen Victoria".' Soon after that last holiday Myra discontinued playing in public and was never able to travel again. During the entire autumn of 1964 and the early months of 1965 I was in London and went to see her almost every other day. Although she was then in the grip of the illness which ended her life, she would still revert to the holiday mood we had shared for nearly four decades. The last night I was in London we dined with friends and when her car came she insisted that since I was leaving the next day, she and Christie, her devoted chauffeur, should drive me to my flat. Our final farewells were said there in her car and although I feel certain that she did not believe in the realization of the plan, we talked hopefully, in those last minutes, of our next holiday together.

Studying With Myra

BY

STEPHEN BISHOP

I N THE spring of 1959 Myra came to give a series of
concerts in San Francisco. Some idea of her popularity
in America can be deduced from the fact that only
Rachmaninov had been asked to make so many appearances
with the San Francisco Symphony in one season. (Six
orchestral concerts plus one recital.) Her playing was
marvellous on the two nights I heard her (Mozart Concerto
in D minor, K.466, and Beethoven No.4 in G): immensely
vital, very dramatic, and technically perfect. She said that
she had only played Beethoven No.4 twice in her life to her
own satisfaction, and I had the incredible luck to hear one of
these performances.

At the time the Griller String Quartet were in residence
at the University of California at Berkeley, and it was
through the kindness of Sidney Griller that I met Myra
after one of her concerts. She very graciously agreed to hear
me play a few days afterwards.

When the time came to play to her I was extremely
nervous, arrived an hour early, and walked around and
around the Sheraton Palace Hotel until it was time for the
appointment. When I walked in she could see how ill at
ease I was, and spent at least half an hour making cheerful conversation, so that when I actually began to play I
was more relaxed than I would have dared to hope. She
agreed to take me as a student, and that summer I came to
London.

It does not follow that a great artist makes a good teacher.
The intensely subjective personality that is necessary for
compelling performance can prove to be awkward when

75

faced with the give and take of teaching. In the music that she knew best—Mozart, Beethoven, Schubert, Schumann, Brahms—Myra was extremely successful in imparting all that she had to offer, yet she remained open to ideas that might be at variance with her own.

The atmosphere at lessons was warm and friendly, and one looked forward to pleasing her, as she was most enthusiastic and encouraging when she felt things were going well. When things were not going well she could be quite devastatingly critical, sometimes making little concession to the fact that one might have to play the work in question at the Wigmore Hall in a few days!

When I first went to her we spent a great deal of time on producing sound. The first piece we worked on was the Brahms-Handel Variations; and in the theme she wanted a quality that was *piano* (Brahms' own marking) yet somehow conveyed that this was the opening of a large work. She imagined the melody as having a small, clear, trumpet-like quality. Her idea of sound was always related to the context of the particular passage, and to the composer: 'You mustn't give a Beethoven *forte* in a Mozart concerto, or a Brahmsian texture to a Beethoven sonata.' This shows something of how her musical mind worked: though her principal concern was the quality of sound she was producing, she never considered it as an end in itself, but arrived at the quality she wanted after considering the piece as a whole.

Part of the reason for her success in producing beautiful and appropriate sound was her way of treating sound-production as a technical problem as well as an exercise for the imagination. She advocated the practice of chords by silent depression of the keys, only gradually increasing the pressure until a perfectly even and *sotto voce* sound was heard, then bringing the volume up to *forte*, thus getting the 'feel' of a chord and enabling you to do what you wanted with it. She had a flair for explaining her way of doing things and once strikingly demonstrated to me the necessity of poised relaxation in tone production by handing me a book, and asking me how I would hold it if I wanted to guess its weight. Of course I held it in an attentive but semi-relaxed way, as by stiffening I would have found it impossible to feel its weight. She then said to apply the same process to feeling the weight of the keys. Another of her technical considerations was to play melodic phrases not from the fingers, but from the back—or at least as far away from the fingers as possible, so that the phrase sounded 'cast in one mould' and the individual notes were not uncontrollably at the mercy of each finger's characteristics.

The most inspiring lessons were on Beethoven, especially late Beethoven. Although she professed no orthodox creed, she had a religious turn of mind, and this was reflected in her deeply moving performances of, and lessons on, Op. 109, 110 and 111. Her knowledge of all the classics from Mozart to Brahms was extensive, and it was here that she was most helpful. Looking back now, the main thing that stands out in her teaching of these composers was her insistence that the performance must have character, and that speed did not necessarily make for exciting playing. She was fond of showing how a tempo in which all the implications of a melody, or the patterns in a bravura passage, could be followed by the ear, actually sounded faster than a quicker tempo in which detail went by too quickly to follow.

By her devotion to music she became a great musician. This same devotion made her an inspiring teacher. Many memorable phrases come to mind: of the opening of the Beethoven G major Concerto; 'Just breathe into the keyboard—all eight notes must sing'; or, in Op. 110, of the inverted re-entry of the fugue subject after the *Arioso dolente*: 'It must be colourless—absolutely white'. But it was her commitment and love of music which remained the basis of her inspiration. I like to remember her by saying after working for hours on some point, 'Now when you perform it, just enjoy the music!' I am very fortunate and grateful to have been helped by this great and delightful person.

Anglo-Dutch Autumn

BY

SIR PAUL MASON

IN THE early autumn of 1954, soon after I had become British Ambassador at The Hague, I learned that Dame Myra Hess would be coming in a few weeks to the Netherlands on a concert tour. I had heard her play many times, and we had even met in the company of friends: but I really hardly knew her. My wife and I agreed, however, that we should try to get her to come and stay with us: so I rang her up as soon as possible, and after establishing my credentials, I said how much we hoped that she would come to us. She was obviously taken somewhat aback and indeed disconcerted by the invitation. She said that she had been coming to Holland regularly for many years, that her visits lasted for three weeks or so, and that she was used to staying at the Hotel des Indes at The Hague where they in turn were used to her requirements. I continued to urge her to come to the Embassy. She said that perhaps I still did not realize the situation. She would have a companion, a relation or a secretary, with her; she would have to practise for hours, and she therefore needed a special sitting room and piano; she had to be free for rehearsals and concerts, and to see friends, and so her movements, and even her meal times, did not fit in easily with normal household routine. I said that I had anticipated all this, that none of it presented any difficulties, and that all we wanted was to have her with us: she could be as free and independent as she chose. I think she was still hesitating a little, when suddenly, 'Very well, thank you very much, I'll come,' she said: and then, with a laugh and in a tone that I was to know so well, she added, 'I feel quite gay.'

78

So began an intimate and devoted friendship which lasted for six happy years in Holland, and then and afterwards in London and Paris up till her last illness and which included, as with Myra it was bound to include, relations and friends on both sides.

But Myra Hess's association with the Netherlands, as she herself had made clear to me, began many years before that first telephone conversation. Indeed, it went back almost to her earliest days as a concert artist. She came first to Amsterdam while still a girl, and spent long periods of time living and working there, not always, at least not at first, as soloist but working with other artists in chamber music, giving and going to concerts, in that most musical of cities, broadening her experience of life (not all the tales she had to tell were wholly happy) and making friends wherever she went. Back she used to come, year after year, becoming increasingly an artist and a person whom the Dutch people took to their hearts. If my memory is correct, the first time that she ever played with Willem Mengelberg (who of course already knew her well) and the Concertgebouw Orchestra was as a last-minute replacement for some artist who had fallen out: but she soon became, and remained, one of his favourites, and she used to tell, with amusement and affection, many stories about that great, if in some ways misguided, personality. On one occasion, though I believe this was in New York, she was playing the Schumann Concerto with him, and at the dress rehearsal he pulled her up sharply during the slow movement and said that her rhythm was so wayward that it made it impossible to accompany her. Having successfully restrained an impulse to burst into tears, Myra was seized with a fit of furious anger, and played through the rest of the rehearsal as if it were a metronomic exercise, deliberately stressing and underlining the pulse to the point of absurdity. She would not look at Mengelberg, though she could feel that he was bristling and that the orchestral players were shaking with suppressed laughter: she flounced off the platform after rehearsal, and went back to her hotel, not knowing if she could bring herself to play that evening. However, her sense of duty came to her help, and she went down to the hall. There was a knock on her dressing-room door: it was Mengelberg. He kissed her hand, thrust a splendid bouquet into her arms, and exclaimed, 'Ach, ach, this evening you play as you wish, I follow you anywhere.'

By the middle nineteen thirties, Myra Hess was to the Dutch people much more than one of the great artists of the day who played regularly up and down the country and could fill any concert hall, however large. Her friends were legion, and there were many families, for instance the Loudon family, to whom she was even more, to whom she was as an honorary aunt or niece or sister. She had lived with them, shared their interests and, if they were musical, made music with them. Many times, in still later years, I used to find, on turning over a volume of music, perhaps Beethoven's Violin Sonatas, in some Dutch house, a page with Myra's signature and a comment such as, 'an afternoon of great musical happiness': and she meant this. And the young people were brought by their parents to meet and hear her just as they, in their turn, were to bring their children.

There is, perhaps, no better proof of the hold which Myra had established over the hearts and the minds of the Dutch than her astonishing experiences immediately after the war of 1939–45. It was the cruellest of wars for that brave people, their Government in exile, their country devastated, their institutions under the heel of a ruthless tyranny, their families often torn apart, themselves starved in body and mind. It was by inspiration that arrangements were made, within hours of the country's liberation, for Myra to be flown over to Holland, where she travelled throughout the country playing to the people in towns and villages, in city halls and village rooms, on every sort and quality of piano, good, indifferent and downright bad. Neither she nor anyone else could speak of this experience without emotion: the thronged audiences so long deprived of an outlet for their feelings: the national anthems sung with everyone in tears. It was exhausting: but it proved without doubt that to the Dutch, as to her own fellow countrymen after the National Gallery Concerts, Myra Hess had become a legend in her own lifetime.

After the war, as she grew older, Myra appeared less on the concert platform abroad, and by the nineteen fifties she had in practice restricted herself to two tours each year: her American tour in the late winter and early spring, and her Dutch tour in the middle of the autumn. Her Dutch tours used to last for about three weeks and, in the last few years at any rate, followed a fairly regular pattern. Using The Hague as a convenient centre, she would normally give three recitals in Amsterdam, The Hague and Rotterdam: one year she gave a recital in Utrecht and another year, instead of solo recitals, she and Isaac Stern played together. She also normally played one concerto in Amsterdam with the Concertgebouw Orchestra and sometimes played twice with them: she also played, during the time I knew her, with orchestras at The Hague, Rotterdam, Utrecht and Maastricht. Her programmes were invariably confined to the great masters: in my time the concertos she played were the second, third and fourth of Beethoven, the second of Brahms and the Schumann. In her recital programmes, she played only Bach, Mozart, Beethoven, Schubert, Schumann and Brahms, except on her final tour when she included Chopin's Funeral March Sonata.

When, in response to the invitation which I have already mentioned, Myra first made her home—I think she would accept the term—with us for one of these tours, we naturally already knew from her devoted Dutch agents Johnny and Johanna Beek, good friends of our own, how long she would be staying, the dates of her concerts and rehearsals and so forth. We were thus able to slip without any preliminary awkwardness into a happy routine which hardly varied, at least in essential matters, in subsequent years. Myra lived in an inter-connecting suite of bedroom, bathroom and sitting room, in the last of which was housed her practice piano. Her niece, Beryl Davis, who to our great pleasure came with her each year, lived across the passage. Myra could thus work, write and see agents or friends quite independently. If she needed to go to Amsterdam or Utrecht to rehearse or look at the piano, the Beeks would take charge of that, and also of escorting her to her concerts unless— which happened in the great majority of cases—we were able to go too. More of that later.

On an ordinary date, that is, one on which no concert or rehearsal immediately impended, Myra would spend the morning in her rooms at practice—to the impairment of the housework, since the maids used to find unexpected and un- necessary tasks to do within earshot of the music. She might be tempted to a mid-morning break for a cup of coffee with my wife to gossip, chain-smoking in a brightly flowered housecoat, and trying to finish *The Times* crossword before I came home to lunch. After lunch she might rest, see a friend or drive out for a little. She would work again after tea, play a game of patience, and then descend at cocktail time ('but alas, only tomato juice, please'). After dinner, she would adore it if one or two friends came to play bridge —definitely not family bridge but a vigorous if somewhat optimistic game: or she might play duets in my study or, on great occasions, play over some of her recital pieces. And so to an early bed.

On a concert day, life went on much as usual till lunch but thereafter things were different. Supposing the concert to be at Amsterdam at 8, it would be necessary to leave The Hague before 7. Myra would perhaps work a little more and then rest for an hour or two, and would have a light meal upstairs before dressing. The big car would draw up, Myra would descend in her cloak with her hair in a scarf, Beryl would bring the music case, and we would pile in. The journey would not be altogether silent, but Myra was always nervous beforehand (what artist is not?) and it was a relief to reach the hall, with Myra received like royalty and a crowd outside, and so away to the artists' room. After the concert and the reception in the artists' room, a cheerful and talkative drive home, with a relaxed Myra chattering about the audience or the orchestra, some supper and this time a not so early bed.

There is so much that I remember about those concerts: apart from the purely musical side, of which I shall say something in a moment, one aspect always remains with me. Myra's coming on stage was unique, both in its dignity and in its friendliness. She was, of course, not a tall woman, and she always wore very full skirts which could have been difficult to manage. Moreover, both the Concertgebouw at Amsterdam and the Concert Hall at The Hague are so built that the artists have to descend, as it were, from the roof down flights of steep steps to the platform in full face of the audience. Down into this packed auditorium (she was one of the three or four artists who could sell out the Concertgebouw days ahead) Myra would advance, holding her skirts in both hands, looking regal, smiling at her audience as if no artist ever felt nervous and no human foot had ever tripped over a skirt or a step. You felt that on arrival on the platform she might sweep you a formal curtsey. Not a bit of it. She just inclined her head three times—were they nods, were they bows?—as if to recognize her audience and to say how glad she was to be with them. And without more ado she sat down.

During the whole time that I knew her, for reasons which I believe, have been given elsewhere,[1] Myra always had the music in front of her at her concerts (there was one exception, after she had had to cancel a number of concerts because of illness, when she tackled without score an immense programme, ending with the Brahms F minor Sonata, with such magnificent gusto that a friend of mine said that she was like someone actually starving for the notes). She tried always to find a young musician to turn pages for her, and as far as I remember she only had to find two in a period

[1] See p. 96 of 'The National Gallery Concerts and After'. (Ed.)

of six years. She delighted in knowing all about their careers and ambitions, and in meeting their wives and children, and they in turn adored her, wrote to her and used to come to greet her and to see her off on leaving Holland.

At the end of each of Myra's visits to us in Holland, when concerts were over and she could relax for a little, we used to give a dinner party for some of the Dutch friends who loved her and her music. This became something of an occasion. Myra would throw aside her self-imposed discipline, consume oysters and champagne and other good things which she adored—'do you think I really ought to? Well, perhaps, just tonight'—and we all basked in her gaiety and radiance. Afterwards, she used to play to us, and none of us will ever forget that music. What music? Perhaps a Bach Partita, or a Schubert Sonata to begin with: after that, anything might happen. On one such evening she began to play Chopin's Black Note Study. A member of the party, sitting some way from the piano, listened judicially to the first few bars, and then whispered to his neighbour, 'The Dame's beginning to lose her technique.' (Myra was then very nearly seventy.) He was not to know that Myra was playing with an orange concealed in the palm of her right hand (a trick she had learned years earlier, I think from Schelling), or that at the cascade of notes at the end, by a prearranged plan she would throw the orange across the piano to me, to the astonishment of her listeners and the delighted discomfiture of her friendly critic. At the end of the evening there was always the inevitable demand for 'Jesu, Joy'—Myra always called it that. No one had much to say afterwards. I think that was how we all wanted to remember Myra. Perhaps it is how we still do.

It was of course not only in Holland that we used to meet. Whenever we were in London, if it was humanly possible, my wife and I used to hurry to Cavendish Close. It was always as if we had hardly been away. Myra would always have Beryl Davis and Howard Ferguson there, so that the fellowship might be complete: and there would be oysters

Photo: Walter Bird, Crown Film Unit

MYRA IN 1942

MYRA WITH SIDNEY GRILLER (left) AND HOWARD FERGUSON, 1942

Photo : Ronald Proctor

for my wife—and for Myra: and perhaps grouse for me,most expertly carved by Howard, and beautifully cooked by the admirable Mrs. Christie: and then an after dinner time of gossip and news of Myra's plans and, in later years, of her pupils and, from us, of her Dutch friends; and finally, as Howard drove us away in his car, Myra kissing her hands to us from the doorstep. I also remember at least one evening alone with her at the theatre. She had chosen the play: it was not a very good one and I think she was a little disappointed by it: but the evening was enlivened by her sardonic, not to say pungent, comments impartially directed at play, performers and audience. There was also a weekend in Paris in 1961 when she and Howard stayed at our flat. It was noisy, the weather blazingly hot, and Myra, already troubled by her hands, was, I think, beginning to feel tired and old. But her gaiety was unquenchable. She had not stayed in Paris for years: so she insisted on packing as much sightseeing as possible into her visit, and on the hottest night of all came with us for a cruise up and down the Seine on a *bâteau-mouche,*where she faced the noisy crowds and what was perhaps one of the worst dinners I have ever eaten with complete aplomb, and indeed with an almost childlike absorption in the colour of the scene and the glow of the floodlit buildings.

While it is not difficult to write about life with Myra, because the details stand out as clearly in my mind as if they belonged to last week, I find it very hard to put into words my thoughts about Myra the person and Myra the musician: if, indeed, the two can be in any way separated. There was a great reserve, and something, too, of shyness, behind the face with which Myra confronted the world: and she would, I am sure, have found it distasteful to think that anyone should try to probe into her personality, or that one should, so to speak, wear her picture upon one's sleeve. I speak of Myra confronting the world. You could not know Myra well without realizing that she was a very brave woman. I am not thinking here of the ultimate loneliness which, whatever the outward circumstances, a life of self dedication must bring. Myra could say something about that in quiet conversation, but it can only be understood, let alone expressed, by those who have taken the same road. I am not even thinking of that burden which led Myra to agree with Casals—and with how many true artists—that to appear in public means the dying of a thousand deaths beforehand. Myra's deep love of her relations, her friends, of everything which made for happy home life was, I am sure, based very largely on her knowledge that her dedication to her calling had made all these things more difficult for her to call her own.

No: when I talk of Myra as a brave woman I am thinking of the gallantry with which she confronted obstacles which, though formidable enough, heaven knows, are more easily comprehensible to most of us. I think, for instance, of her hands. I could almost say that I hardly knew Myra when she was not having trouble with her hands which, I suppose, is somewhat like thinking of Atalanta having trouble with her tendon Achilles. Those miraculous instruments of her calling—but in the first place, they were so small. I used to be amazed at the splendour of her playing of the tremendous Second Piano Concerto of Brahms. How could she ever encompass the monumental technical requirements of the first two movements? Indeed, she used sometimes to speak of this in her own uniquely humorous way. Somewhere along her Dutch trail, she had come across a phrase which ran, if I remember aright, 'Scrubble op de beestje', which is, I think, intended to describe a very short rider trying to mount without stirrups a very tall horse. At least, that is how Myra took it: and while she used it to describe her handling of the technical problems set by Brahms, and perhaps by other composers, she characteristically broadened it to cover any difficulties which came her way.

But those small hands of hers were for ever troubling Myra: the skin of the fingers would split and crack and make playing an agony. Just before one of her visits to Holland,

86

she had a crack near a nail, and was given a penicillin injection to heal it. But neither she nor the doctor realized that she was allergic to penicillin, and the morning after her arrival at The Hague, she woke up with a fierce temperature, her face so swollen that her eyes could barely see or be seen and with huge swellings, to use her own phrase, 'in all the possible and impossible places'. The rash and fever were slow to cure: and, besides being in great pain and discomfort, she had to cancel all but the last handful of her Dutch concerts which, for Myra, was far worse than any possible physical discomfort. She not only never complained, she made jokes about her sorry condition. That was Myra all over. Those same hands, as time went on, were progressively attacked by rheumatism and arthritis till, not only did public appearances become agony for her but, when she retired, she was deprived of the joy to which she had always looked forward, that of playing, as she used to say, 'as an amateur' for her own pleasure and the enjoyment of her friends. This also she bore with resignation. That, too, was Myra.

This serenity of spirit was something else which, in thinking of Myra, one immediately thinks of also. I am far from meaning that she could never get ruffled, or upset, or cross. I have seen her get very impatient at careless mismanagement, and very much put out if things were done in a slovenly way: she could be very critical of professional incompetence (though she could speak almost affectionately of an orchestra, not quite in the front rank, as 'having more spit than polish'); she could be scathing of anything pretentious and undeniably feminine in discussing personalities. Her serenity was invigorating, not disarming. You did not go to her to be soothed but to be braced. This serenity of spirit may have been hard won. I remember once reading of a pianist who shall be nameless, that his performance 'had the hallmark of a fine musicianship which has solved its problems'. That could indeed have been said of Myra the woman. Her serenity of spirit had solved its problems.

And what of Myra the musician? What indeed can a layman say? That she loved to foster and encourage music in all its forms, provided that those who made it truly loved it: that is true. She could say to you, 'you made your piano sound beautiful this evening', and you would hold your head high ever afterwards. She could play with enthusiastic amateurs and write afterwards, as I have said, on their score, 'an afternoon of great musical happiness', and you knew that it had been true for her, as for them. These are humble illustrations of the humility and enthusiasm with which she placed her wonderful gifts at the disposal of all who truly sought for them. Of those gifts themselves I shall dare to take two aspects and to illustrate them from her Dutch tours and the many friends there who loved to honour and acclaim her.

First of all I think of Myra's sense, her supreme sense, of presentation; by which I mean the power to state something in terms which are forward looking and outward looking to the accomplishment of the structure which is to be built. I remember a recital at The Hague, at which Myra played Schumann's *Carnaval*. As she came to the end of the Preambule, a dear old friend, with whom Myra loved to make music, whispered to me, 'See, how wonderfully she sets the stage for the entrance of her characters.' When Myra began to play, you felt that from the first note, and indeed before that, she saw with absolute clearness how the work would, indeed must, unfold: and though I suppose this is what all artists strive for, not all achieve it. For me, it made Myra's playing immensely exciting, a word not often used about it. I used to think of the poet's words, 'In my beginning is my ending'. Myra always made one realize how true that is.

The Dutch are an immensely music-loving people, and I daresay it would be true to say that a typical Dutch concert audience contains more people than any other audience for whom music, whether they play, teach or write about it, is at the centre of their lives. They would of course react in different ways to Myra's playing, depending upon what it was that struck closest home to them. I remember a friend who always spoke with emotion about Myra's *noble* left hand. Another—I think this was after some Schubert—said that no one else understood so profoundly the relationship between silence and sound and the value which each gave to each. Others would dwell on her exact sense of style: and so on. But I think that the essence of their feeling about it all, and this was what drew them so intensely to her, could be summed up as follows: 'So often we go to a concert to hear so-and-so: with Dame Myra we go to hear the music.'

Whenever she came, and whatever else she chose, in Holland Myra always played Beethoven. This was in itself a passport to Dutch favour: for she made it quite clear that, for her as for them, among the great Beethoven was the greatest. One year her recital programme consisted of the three last sonatas, Opus 111 being played after the interval. I do not know whether, or how often, this had been done before in Holland. It is very moving to remember that tour, and very difficult to describe it. I think that Myra was herself very much moved by the experience. The halls were, as always, packed, and the audiences, as always, hung on the music. But this time things were different. People went away quietly at the end and neither they, nor after them the critics, seemed to find it very easy to comment. But I know that those evenings have not been forgotten.

Myra Hess loved Holland and the Dutch people and was happy with and among them for many reasons: but perhaps above all because she knew that there was no reserve between them and her in their common trust in the healing power of great music.

After one of the Beethoven evenings my wife asked Myra, as we were driving home together, whether she understood what Beethoven was trying to say in his last works. Myra reflected for a little, and then, in her gentle voice, she replied: 'No: but I think Beethoven would understand what I have been trying to do when I play them.' I expect he has told her so.

The National Gallery Concerts and After

BY

HOWARD FERGUSON

IF MYRA Hess had been asked what was the most remarkable episode in her life, there is little doubt that she would have replied 'The National Gallery Concerts.' In order to appreciate this, two facts must be borne in mind. Firstly, that when war was declared on 3 September 1939 Myra immediately cancelled an extensive American tour, feeling that her place was in her own country, even if at the moment she had little idea what she could do there. And secondly, all theatres, cinemas and concert halls in London had been closed by order of the Home Office; museums and galleries were emptied of their treasures, as Sir Kenneth Clark recounts; and Londoners were left, in the intervals of putting up black-out curtains and evacuating children to the country, to meditate on their possible fate. Though such restrictions were doubtless necessary in the initial emergency, they could not remain in force indefinitely, for people required mental and spiritual stimulus as well as food. No one felt this more strongly than Myra, who became increasingly convinced, as those strange, unreal September days of the 'phoney war' passed by, that countless people were being starved of music and that she must try to do something about it.

While spending a late-September weekend in Surrey with her old teacher Tobias Matthay, she spoke of this and asked the other members of the party whether they thought it might be possible to arrange some concerts? If so, where could they be given?

'Why not in the National Gallery?' asked the irrepressibly optimistic Denise Lassimonne.

'Or perhaps in Buckingham Palace!' replied the less sanguine Myra.

Yet surprisingly enough, Denise's unlikely idea bore fruit. The Director of the National Gallery, Sir Kenneth Clark, was approached and enthusiastically agreed that since pictures could no longer be seen there, it was wholly appropriate that music should be heard daily instead. A small committee was formed, including Myra, Sir Kenneth and Mr. Frank Howes; permission to hold the Concerts was obtained from the Trustees of the Gallery and the Office of Works; and the Home Office agreed to relax the ban forbidding crowds to gather in public buildings. It was then announced in the press and on the radio that a series of lunchtime Concerts of chamber music would take place in the National Gallery from Mondays to Fridays at 1 p.m., with a repeat of the Tuesday and Friday programmes at 4.30 (these afternoon concerts were discontinued after two-and-a-half months). Admission would be one shilling; and any profits would go to The Musicians' Benevolent Fund, for the profession had been hard hit by the cessation of concert-giving throughout the country.

Five days later, on Tuesday 10 October 1939, Myra herself gave the first concert—'in case the whole thing is a flop', as she put it. She need not have worried. Long before the doors opened a line of people stretched down the steps of the Gallery and round the far corner of Trafalgar Square; and by the time the doors had to be closed on the disappointed tail-end of the queue, roughly a thousand people had crowded in. (The Home Office had given permission for an audience of two hundred.) More than half had to stand; but all listened entranced to a programme of Scarlatti, Bach, Beethoven, Schubert, Chopin and Brahms; and from that moment Myra's dream of providing music daily for whoever wished to hear it became a practical reality.

No one had expected such an overwhelming response.

Thinking that only a few dozen of her friends might turn up, Myra had asked Beryl Davis, her niece and faithful war-time secretary, to take the money at the door. When the flood of people poured in, poor Beryl was almost submerged. Worse still, she found she had no change for the first person in the queue, who happened to present a half-crown for his shilling ticket. The Concerts had started literally with nothing in the till.

The continued success of such a venture depended, of course, on the goodwill and co-operation of the entire musical profession. This never failed. Every artist, from the most famous to the youngest recruit, came for a flat-rate token fee in recognition of the fact that they were helping a splendid cause. And Myra felt that she could ask this of her colleagues, not only because she herself accepted nothing whatever for any work connected with the Concerts, but also because artists were only booked a few weeks in advance, so that an appearance at the Gallery never meant the loss of a more lucrative engagement.

After a few weeks Sir Kenneth Clark was approached by Lady Gater with the brilliant suggestion of a Canteen for the Concert audiences. The Committee were delighted at the idea, for besides solving the difficulty of the visitor who was unable to bring his own lunch, it would perhaps reduce the ubiquitous rustling of sandwich-paper which at times threatened to drown the music. Soon Lady Gater and her helpers were providing music-lovers and others with the best sandwiches in London, and her Canteen was making substantial and very welcome contributions to The Musicians' Benevolent Fund.

From the outset Myra's aim had been twofold: to present the complete literature of first-rate chamber music at a price that all could afford; and to give young and promising performers an opportunity of appearing before a ready-made audience, side by side with already established artists. Chamber music of every kind, instrumental and vocal, plus a certain amount of music for small orchestra, constituted the hour-

long programmes. Sometimes they were devoted to works
by a single composer—oddly enough these always drew a
larger audience than equivalent mixed programmes—the
most popular being Beethoven, Mozart and Bach, in that
order. Various series were given from time to time, such as
the complete chamber works of Beethoven and Brahms; the
Bach Forty-eight Preludes & Fugues and Brandenburg Concertos; and the twenty-one Mozart Piano Concertos, played
by Myra herself. Many lesser-known works were also included—it must be remembered that this was long before
the B.B.C. Third Programme—such as the wind Serenades of
Mozart and Beethoven, Schütz's 'Christmas Oratorio', Bach's
'Art of Fugue' and 'Musical Offering', and the Church
Sonatas of Mozart. A highly successful innovation was the
the series of lecture-recitals on all the Beethoven Quartets,
given more than once by Ivor James with the assistance of
the Menges String Quartet. Miniature scores of these and
of other works were always on sale at the door, and were
snapped up as quickly as the publishers could supply them.

The programmes themselves were planned about a month
in advance by Myra and myself. (When the Concerts finally
came to an end she said to me, 'Isn't it extraordinary? During six-and-a-half years' incessant work together we've
never actually hit one another!') They were then passed on
to Messrs. Ibbs & Tillett, the concert agents, who booked
the artists for us and made all arrangements for printing
and advertising. Weekly programmes were on sale at the
Gallery and elsewhere—they became smaller and smaller
as the paper shortage grew more acute—and more detailed
programmes were available for each day's concert. These
and statistical records of every aspect of the Concerts were
carefully kept by Beryl Davis; and as they formed a uniquely
comprehensive view of the whole scheme, were eventually
bound up in a series of volumes and bequeathed by Myra
to the British Museum.

Audiences varied between 250 and 1,750 daily, depending on such factors as the war news, the weather, the type

of programme (a solo pianist drew more than a string quartet, and a singer less than either), the eminence of the performer, and even the day of the week. A forecast of the attendance at every Concert had to be made a week in advance to guide the Canteen in their sandwich-making; and this task, partaking equally of experience and black magic, was also undertaken by Beryl, who became so expert that she could tell to within fifty the size of audience that any programme would bring.

Needless to say, smooth organization was not achieved in a day, nor was it maintained without incident through all the vicissitudes of war, even though the Concerts could eventually make the proud boast, in company with the famous girl-show at the Windmill Theatre, that they had never once closed down. Myra had no experience as an organizer, and had never even served on a committee before. At the first meeting Sir Kenneth asked would she take the chair. 'If I must,' she replied; then added, after sitting down, 'What do we do next—move around one, like the Mad Hatter's tea-party?' She possessed, nevertheless, three invaluable qualifications for this unfamiliar work: she knew exactly what she wanted; she did not mind how much trouble she took to achieve it; and she was able, with an irresistible combination of humour and urgency, to charm almost anything out of anybody.

She used to say that her greatest achievement had been to wheedle permission from some reluctant official to buy protective wire-netting for the glass roof of the Gallery 'with the bribe of an orange'. (This was when oranges were unobtainable in the shops.) The strict accuracy of her description may be doubted; but it is certainly true that when military bands were threatened in Trafalgar Square during the concert hour, she averted what would have been an impossible uproar by agreeing to make an appeal for War Savings from a bomber-plane placed in the Square.

Other crises were more serious and unavoidable. The daylight air-raids of the Battle of Britain made it necessary, in

September 1940, to move the Concerts from the glass-roofed Dome to the downstairs Shelter-room, where greater safety was to be found at the expense of comfort and space. With the intensive night-raids of winter 1940–41 difficulties increased daily. Audiences and performers alike would pick their way through glass-strewn streets flanked by smouldering buildings, to find the Gallery miraculously still standing, though scarred and without heating of any kind. The Shelter, which in September had seemed so airless, developed an unbelievable number of piercing draughts; and large pools of water collected on the stone floor, in spite of the tireless efforts of the faithful Mr. Smith, the wartime Head Attendant at the Gallery. The cold became intense. Performers battled with blue fingers, helped only by a couple of oil-stoves on the platform, while the audience wrapped themselves in rugs and top coats. Yet in spite of everything, both audience and performers continued to turn up unfailingly.

At 11 o'clock on the morning of 15 October 1940, Myra was told on the phone that a time-bomb had fallen on the Gallery and that the building must be evacuated immediately. Half an hour later the High Commissioner for South Africa had generously placed at her disposal the Library in nearby South Africa House; so, time-bomb or no, that day's Concert took place after all, and for the only occasion outside the National Gallery. On returning to the Gallery another time-bomb was found buried in wreckage; so the Concerts were hurriedly moved to a room in the most distant part of the building. A couple of days later, in the lunch-hour and in the middle of a Beethoven String Quartet, the bomb went off with a terrific explosion. By a miracle nobody was hurt; and as the Shelter escaped with only broken windows, the Concerts were able to return there once more.

With the decrease in raids it became possible in June 1941 to move the Concerts back to their original home under the Dome. It was a double relief, for the nine months of

restricted accommodation in the Shelter, and the conse-
quently diminished audiences, had put a severe strain on
their financial resources. Indeed, it is not at all certain that
they could have continued had it not been for a timely gift
of over £4,000 from the United States. This magnificent sum
was contributed by Myra's countless American friends and
admirers as a token of appreciation for all that she had done
and was doing for music and her country. The appeal was
organized by Professor Arthur Mendel, and donors included
Toscanini, Koussevitsky, Rachmaninov, Heifetz, and many
other world famous musicians.

Meanwhile, of course, Myra herself was playing continually. Though she limited the number of her outside engagements to a considerable extent, she was appearing in
public a great deal. At the National Gallery alone, where
she could always guarantee a full house, she played no less
than 146 times; and, as can be seen from the list beginning
on p. 109, she took part in an enormous amount of chamber
music, all involving much rehearsal. She even found time
to learn some entirely new works, such as my own Piano
Sonata and Bagatelles, and many unfamiliar ones, like the
dozen or more Mozart Concertos she had never played
before. These last were a tremendous undertaking. They
were usually given in pairs, with Alec Sherman and his New
London Orchestra; and invariably on the evening before
each performance I would go round to her house in Wildwood Road, where we were near neighbours, to play through
the works on two pianos. Once, when she was more than usually tired, my friend Arnold van Wyk came with me to turn
pages. The unfamiliar E flat Concerto, K.449, sounded somewhat sketchy to put it mildly; and as Arnold and I walked
home in the blackout afterwards he said to me in awe-struck
tones, 'My Gawd! . . . and she's going to play it tomorrow!'
Yet when tomorrow came, Myra sailed through the work
as though she had known it all her life.

During the war years she began to play from music
occasionally in public. It started with the Mozart Concertos,

which she felt were essentially chamber music. She then began to extend the practice to certain other concertos and to some solo works, as she found it saved a lot of nervous wear-and-tear that she could ill afford. At first she was a little shy about it, and would explain to the audience that it was *not* because she hadn't done enough work: it was merely because in this way she would be able to enjoy herself more, and hoped therefore that they would do the same. But gradually she and everbody else accepted the presence of a score as quite normal—as indeed it always was until the mid-nineteenth century—and she felt free for the rest of her life to use it whenever she felt inclined, even if there were certain works, such as the Beethoven G major Concerto and the Schumann, that she always played from memory. I often turned pages for her, and would notice how rarely she even glanced at the music. It was, indeed, more of a reassurance than a necessity, and one which she often wished other performers would allow themselves whenever they found memory-playing a strain.

The Concerts at the Gallery continued with unabated success after their return to the Dome, and without further interruption until the flying-bomb attacks in the summer of 1944 made a temporary return to the Shelter advisable. Luckily this lasted only three months, as the Gallery escaped damage both then and during the later rocket attacks.

The fifth anniversary of the Concerts was marked by the publication of a booklet containing contributions from Myra, Sir Kenneth, and Mr. E. M. Forster ('From the Audience'), besides a short account of their history, and lists of all the artists who had taken part and of the works performed. The range of programmes can be judged from the fact that the latter filled sixty pages of double-columned print.

With the beginning of the liberation of Europe came the first intoxicating visits of performers from abroad. Francis Poulenc and Pierre Bernac were the earliest to arrive, bringing with them an unknown young violinist called Ginette Neveu, whose masterly playing made a profound impression on audiences at the Gallery and elsewhere. Nor was the traffic in one direction only. Myra herself was invited to return to Holland even before the fighting there had finished; and this proved to be one of the most moving experiences of her life, for she was greeted not only as a beloved, long-lost friend, but also as a near-miraculous proof of the country's ever-growing freedom.

This period also brought its problems. As the foreseeable end of the war in Europe drew nearer, Myra became increasingly concerned about the future of the Concerts. They so clearly filled a need in the musical life of the nation, for audiences and young musicians alike, that she was extremely anxious to see them established on a permanent footing. So much so, that she was perfectly willing to accept the partial sacrifice of the rest of her career, provided the Trustees of the Gallery agreed to the Concerts continuing there indefinitely. (A move would have been impractical, for no other suitable building could be found in the neighbourhood, or indeed elsewhere.) The conjunction of music and painting seemed particularly happy; and though the initial period of post-war reorganization might present difficulties, they surely need not prove insurmountable? A memorandum outlining a possible scheme was forwarded to the Trustees by Sir Kenneth with his blessing, though he himself would soon be leaving the Gallery; as a result it was agreed that the Concerts should continue in the Dome for another year at least, and that the position should then be reviewed.

This renewed proof of the Trustees' appreciation was encouraging. But as peace came to Europe and 1945 drew to a close, Myra felt that she would soon have to know one way or the other about the future; for America was clamouring for her long-postponed return and could not wait indefinitely for a yes or a no. At the beginning of 1946 she therefore asked the Chairman of the Trustees, Mr. Vincent Massey, for a firm decision. On 14 February, while in Oxford to give a recital, she heard by phone that the Trustees had decided it was not going to be possible to continue the Concerts, because of the reconstruction work that was planned for restoring the building. This was a bitter blow. And it was not lessened when, on her return to town, she read a press-release from the Gallery which stated that Dame Myra would be retiring from the direction of the Concerts, and went on to express the Board's 'sincere regret that it was found impossible to continue the Concerts permanently after her retirement'. As there had never been any question of Myra retiring from the direction of the Concerts—a fact which she had made very clear to Mr. Massey in a letter written a fortnight earlier—the Concert Committee felt bound to ask that this mis-statement should be corrected in the Gallery's records.

The date chosen for the final programme was 10 April 1946, which meant that the Concerts had run without a break for exactly six-and-a-half years. At it the Griller String Quartet rounded off their many appearances at the Gallery by playing works by Haydn and Beethoven—surely an appropriate note on which to bring the Concerts to a close, as a string quartet is the most perfect form of chamber music, and chamber music was what Myra had so long ago determined to provide.

Thus an extraordinary and imaginative adventure came to an end. In all 1,698 Concerts had been given, in which the number of performers taking part totalled 238 different pianists, 236 string players, 64 wind players, 157 singers, 24 string quartets and 56 other ensembles, besides 13 orchestras, 15 choirs, and 24 conductors. Over £23,000 had been paid in artists' fees; more than £16,000 had been contributed to The Musicians' Benevolent Fund; and over three-quarters-of-a-million people had come to listen to chamber music —the exact number was 824,152. Every section of the community had been represented in the audiences. Her Majesty the Queen, now Queen Elizabeth the Queen Mother, honoured the Concerts with her presence on several occasions, sometimes bringing with her the young Princess Elizabeth, our present Queen, and her sister Princess Margaret.

Music-lovers of every description, civilian and service, came either regularly or whenever they could find an opportunity. And many who had never in their lives thought of listening to serious music dropped in by chance, enjoyed what they heard (often to their surprise), and returned again and again.

Public gratitude for all that Myra had done and stood for, as well as for her unique contribution as a pianist, found expression in a variety of ways. In 1941 she was promoted in the Order of the British Empire from Commander to Dame, and a year later was presented with the Gold Medal of the Royal Philharmonic Society. She was also made a Commander of the Order of Orange Nassau by Queen Wilhelmina of Holland, and received honorary doctorates from the Universities of Durham, London, Cambridge, Manchester, Leeds, St. Andrews and Reading.

The war years undoubtedly had an influence on Myra's playing, for her powers of interpretation from then onwards seemed to acquire a new simplicity, directness and depth. Inessentials fell away, partly because the pressure of her life and the circumstances of wartime combined to sharpen perception, and partly because she never stopped developing as a musician. It became hard to imagine that there was once a time when, as Denise Lassimonne recounts, 'little Hess always bolted and lost control', though such a possibility was sometimes believable in the pre-war years. Where earlier her quest for sheer beauty of sound might at times distort the larger view of the music she was performing, she later had such complete tonal control that she was able to concentrate on the music's shape and meaning, secure in the knowledge that her fingers would reproduce exactly what her inner ear dictated. She had a remarkably sure instinct which became finer and finer with the passing years; and though she was not what one thinks of as an intellectual player, she had an unerring faculty for reaching the heart of whatever music awoke her love and interest. Her earliest ambition had been to play late Beethoven; and latterly, when the last

Photo: Associated Press

MYRA WITH TOBIAS MATTHAY ON HIS 85th BIRTHDAY, 1943

MYRA WITH BRUNO WALTER IN NEW YORK, 1956

three sonatas often appeared in her programmes, one felt that her imagination comprehended their remote world as fully as her superb control of the keyboard enabled her to reveal it to the listener. Like Schnabel, she invariably convinced one that Schubert's 'heavenly lengths' were truly heaven-sent; and like no one else I have heard, she could maintain that knife-edge balance between gaiety and heart-break that is the very essence of Mozart.

Her platform personality was striking. When she seated herself at the keyboard her apparent serenity was so marked that few people could believe what an abyss of nervous uncertainty it hid. Yet in spite of the agonies she suffered before every concert, the moment she stepped on the platform she made the audience feel that they were her friends, and that the only thing that mattered was the music they were going to enjoy together.

Myra always used to say that she was as strong as a horse—and so indeed she must have been to survive the strenuous life she led. But during the post-war years she had a number of serious illnesses, the cumulative effect of which must be borne in mind if we are to understand the sad and wholly unexpected aftermath of her retirement.

While appearing in Boston in 1950 she suffered an attack of hepatitis (she always referred to it as 'hippopotamus'), which meant weeks in bed and the cancellation of the rest of her tour. Three years later her concerts in the States were again cut short when her gall-bladder had to be removed in an emergency operation in Chicago. Devoted care and her own strong constitution pulled her through these two illnesses without apparent after-effects. But in 1960, when she was 70 years old, she had a coronary thrombosis not long before she was due to leave England for another of her American tours. She appeared to weather it safely; but shortly after one of her New York concerts she had another thrombosis, this time in the neck, when her powers of movement were partly, if only temporarily, affected. In spite of this, she felt able to play again on her return to England

and looked forward to many more appearances in public. During the whole of this time an added complication was her tendency to arthritis. So long as she was continually playing it could be kept under control; but during illness, when she was unable to practise, it inevitably gained a foothold—or rather a handhold, for that was where it mattered most. In addition, she was never wholly free from arterial and circulatory troubles from 1960 onwards. It is scarcely surprising, therefore, if her last public appearance was at the Festival Hall on 31 October 1961, when she played the Mozart A major Concerto, K.488, under Sir Adrian Boult. The concert was a singularly appropriate one, for it commemorated the 21st anniversary of the Battle of Britain, and Myra had played the same work almost exactly 21 years before with the R.A.F. Orchestra at one of the National Gallery Concerts. As she was still uncertain about the state of her hands, no mention of her possible retirement was made; and in fact she later did a live broadcast of the Schubert B flat posthumous Sonata, and a recorded one of the Haydn Sonata No. 52 in E flat. She then decided that this must be the end.

In the past Myra had often thought how wonderful it would be when she retired and need no longer face the strain of the next concert. She would then be able to cut her hair—dressing it had always been a maddening business—and play for her own pleasure all the music for which there had hitherto been too little time.

Alas, it did not work out like that. Though she found some satisfaction in once more picking up the threads of teaching—Stephen Bishop writes on p. 75 of their work together—she lacked the physical stamina to take enough pupils to engage her time and interest fully. Nor had she any inclination to play now that her hands had grown so painful. Reading, radio and the gramophone all required too much concentration; and even her friends could do little to help, for they sensed after an hour or so that she found the effort of maintaining contact too tiring. She herself felt as if she were constantly under an anaesthetic; and the only defences she had against annihilating boredom were sleep, watching tennis and show-jumping on TV, an occasional hand of canasta or backgammon, and endless solitary games of patience. Life had unaccountably become a desert, and each morning brought anew the fearful problem of how in the world she was going to get through the day.

What was the reason for this melancholy change? Professor Mendel suggests a possible explanation on p. 40; but the medical evidence, hitherto little known outside her immediate circle, showed that the cause was physical. After her second thrombosis of early 1961 in New York the doctors knew that there had been brain damage, and that this was bound to make itself felt increasingly with the passing of time. It was, indeed, only her extraordinary determination and courage that enabled her to conquer such a disability for a while and appear again in public. (It is altogether typical that as late as 1964 she should have faced the ordeal of a two-hour operation on her neck, to clear an artery, with only a local anaesthetic.) Myra certainly never lacked courage or the ability to face facts, however unpleasant. It is unthinkable, therefore, that she would have been incapable of accepting and making the best of her retirement, had she been her normal self or anything like it. Unfortunately for her own peace of mind she was very far from that.

Irene Scharrer has written of Myra's willingness to sacrifice everything for her music. If the last bleak years were part of the price she had to pay, she never for a moment complained; and we, who have benefited so immeasurably by her single-mindedness, can only marvel and be humbly grateful that it was so. She was richly gifted, and she gave richly of her gifts: for besides being a great pianist, she was a great, rare, warm-hearted, generous and intensely loveable human being.

The Presentation of Honorary Degrees: Cambridge, 9 June 1949

Citation by the Public Orator, Dr W.K.C. Guthrie

PHILOSOPHIAE litterarumque dotes in magno pretio habere nos Cantabrigienses, debitam observantiam viris feminisque doctis adhibere velle, ab omnibus, puto, concedetur. Ignoscent igitur mihi ceteri hospites egregii si confiteor illam, quae seriem nostram hodie claudit, plurium animos arte sua recreasse videri, pluribus oblectamenta vitae hodiernae et miseriarum solacia attulisse, quam maior pars eorum qui propter scientiam vel eruditionem magnum nomen habent. Etenim multitudinum innumerabilium auribus hic inter nos (nam nobis diu familiaris est), in Batavia, in America, in aliis orbis terrarum partibus, tactu chordarum mirabili blandita est et corda permulsit; quod vero quovis tempore mortalium generi beneficium haud leve ducendum est. Quid igitur quod sine huius unius constantia et labore benevolo vix ulla Londiniensibus occasio data esset, ut belli molestiis per quinquennium obtusi et periculis circumdati 'aliquem fructum caperent dulcedinis almae' et gloriosorum illorum (quos dicit liber Ecclesiasticus) operibus delectarentur, qui modos musicos exquisissent? Malebat enim easdem molestias ipsa perferre, pericula perpeti, quam suos tum, cum ope tali maxime egerent, deserere. Sed quid valuerint symphoniae illae meridianae dactylographorum humillima, quae eas celebrabant, melius quam ego exprimere potest. Ad summam—nam de singulis agere vetamur imperiti—nulla ambitione adducta artem quam habet perfectam ex mero Musarum amore et erga homines caritate ad felicitatem aliorum augendam exercet.

Duco ad vos Excellentissimi Ordinis Imperi Britannici Dominam Commendatricem,

MYRAM HESS.

The Presentation of Honorary Degrees

(translation)

I do not think that we can be accused in Cambridge of setting too low a value on the gifts of philosophy or literature, nor of denying to men and women of learning the respect which is their due. Our other illustrious guests will therefore pardon me, I hope, if I confess to the belief that she who comes last on our list has by her art been able to give spiritual refreshment to a greater number of people, to convey more pleasure, more solace in the hardships and anxieties of present-day life, than most of those who have won a name in science or scholarship. By her magic touch she has charmed the ears and warmed the hearts of thousands—here among us (for she is an old friend in Cambridge), in Holland, in America, and in many other countries. And this would surely be accounted at any time no small service to the human race. It is even more, when we remember that without her faithfulness and loving labour the workers of London, when the perils of war pressed hard upon them, would have had practically no opportunity of relaxing in hard-won enjoyment of the works of those famous men who, as Ecclesiasticus has it, 'sought out musical tunes'. She preferred to share the dangers and inconvenience of their life, rather than desert her own people at a time when they were in especial need of the solace which she, above all others, knew how to provide. How much those midday concerts meant, the humblest shorthand typist who attended them could testify better than I. In short (for my ignorance prevents me from recounting the details of her skill), she is one completely unambitious for herself, who out of sheer love of music and warmth of human feeling exercises her art to the greater happiness of others.

I present to you

MYRA HESS

Dame Commander of the Most Excellent Order of the British Empire

Doctor of Music (*honoris causa*)

105

Myra Hess

Dame Myra's reply on behalf of the Honorary Graduates at the Luncheon following the Ceremony

Chancellor, Vice-Chancellor, my Lords, Ladies and Gentlemen, I always view the prospect of speaking in public with profound trepidation: indeed, had I known my fate a week ago, I would undoubtedly have spent the entire journey from America pacing the decks of the Mauretania, rehearsing a speech instead of spending a good many hours, as I did, playing innumerable games of ping-pong.

However, my acceptance of the invitation to reply to the toast of the honorary graduates, made by the well-beloved Chancellor [Field-Marshal Smuts], was given without hesitation when I realized that in this year of all years it was fitting that the response should be made by a woman. For I understand that it is only recently that we women have been admitted to full membership of the University.

Cambridge may be justly proud of having appointed a woman professor before Oxford took such a bold step: but there must have been a certain uneasiness in many minds about the equivocal position of this distinguished lady. Now that this has been rectified, I am sure it must be gratifying to Professor Garrod and to countless others to know that their University has at length—if I may so put it—made honest women of them.

This has been a seemingly light-hearted prelude, but I should like to say most seriously how deeply honoured I feel to be among the first women to be made honorary graduates of Cambridge University, for which I have so great a reverence and affection.[1] Keen though my own personal pleasure is at receiving this honour, it is a still deeper gratification to think that the gesture has been made to the musical profession, or rather to music itself. For I believe that in recent years music has begun to take

[1] Queen Elizabeth, now Queen Elizabeth the Queen Mother, was the first woman to receive an honorary degree at Cambridge; Dame Myra was the second. (Ed.)

its place as a vitally important element in the life of the community. I say begun, because we have not yet found a wholly satisfactory way of presenting music so that it shall be available for all who may want to hear it. During the war, my experience at the National Gallery and elsewhere was a revelation. It proved beyond doubt how real was the need for music in the lives of people in almost every walk of life. Day after day many hundreds would come to hear programmes of Beethoven Quartets, Bach Cantatas, and all that was best in chamber music; and to many of them the enjoyment of music opened up wholly unsuspected horizons.

Typical of this was a young sailor who strolled into the National Gallery by chance one day. After the war I happened to meet him, now a civilian, and he shyly told me his story. He said, 'Me and a pal was walking round Trafalgar Square on our 'alf day's leave. We saw there was a concert and thought we would see what it was like. We went in, you was playing that day, Miss, and a damned good show it was!' He then told me that by the end of the war six of them, Petty-Officers, whenever they had a day's leave, would never miss an opportunity of coming to the concerts.

This is only one instance of what must have happened thousands of times. The opportunity then existed for people to discover that something had been missing from their lives; nobody told them that a Beethoven or a Mozart Quartet was high-brow, or beyond their understanding; they just sat back, listened, and a new world opened to them.

Since Elizabethan days there has probably never been such a demand for serious music as there is today. Not only in England, but all over the world it is evident that this demand cannot be satisfied by the conventional series of concerts, which financially are beyond the great majority of people. Yet how important it is that a way should be found to enlarge the scope of public music-making. In times as unsettled as our own, music can have a profound influence for good. It is unfettered by the barrier of words, and needs no translation; and therefore it is one of the great forces that can bring people together in mind and spirit.

How is this consummation to be achieved? At the moment it is difficult to give the answer. We must hope that the forces of habit and prejudice in the musical world will gradually give way to a more enlightened view of our present needs. This reformation may take time; but perhaps it will come about in the same happy way in which this University has found it possible to reconcile tradition with the claims of emancipated womanhood.

And now, not only for myself but also on behalf of my distinguished colleagues, may I express my heartfelt appreciation to the Chancellor for his very kind words of welcome today, and to the University for the great honour they have bestowed on us.

Works played by Myra Hess at the National Gallery Concerts

A. Arensky
Valse, for two pianos

J. S. Bach
Forty-eight Preludes and Fugues:
   3. C sharp minor
  21. B flat
  22. B flat minor
Prelude in G, S.902
Toccata in D
French Suite No. 5 in G
Partita No. 1 in B flat
Italian Concerto
Adagio in G, S.968
Chorale: 'Jesu, Joy of Man's Desiring' (arr. Hess)
Concerto No. 1 in D minor
Concerto No. 5 in F minor
Brandenburg Concerto No. 5 in D
Concerto in C for two pianos
Concerto in C minor for two pianos
Sonata in E flat for two pianos (arr. Keller)
'Sheep may Safely Graze' for two pianos (arr. Howe)
Sonatas for Violin and Piano:
  1. B minor
  2. A
  3. E
  4. C minor
  5. F minor
  6. G

L. van Beethoven
Sonatas:
  3. C, Op. 2, No. 3
  8. C minor, Op. 13
 14. C sharp minor, Op. 27, No. 2
 17. D minor, Op. 31, No. 2
 23. F minor, Op. 57
 31. A flat, Op. 110
 32. C minor, Op. 111
Six Variations, Op. 34
Rondo in G, Op. 51, No. 2
Sonatas for Violin and Piano:
  1. D, Op. 12, No. 1
  2. A, Op. 12, No. 2
  3. E flat, Op. 12, No. 3
  4. A minor, Op. 23
  5. F, Op. 24
  6. A, Op. 30, No. 1
  7. C minor, Op. 30, No. 2
  8. G, Op. 30, No. 3
  9. A, Op. 47
 10. G, Op, 96
Sonatas for Cello and Piano:
  2. G minor, Op. 5, No. 2
  3. A, Op. 69
Piano Trios:
  3. C minor, Op. 1, No. 3
  5. D, Op. 70, No. 1
  7. B flat, Op. 97
  8. B flat, Op. posth.

E. Bloch
Piano Quintet

J. Brahms
Sonata No. 3 in F minor, Op. 5
Capriccio in D minor, Op. 116, No. 7
Intermezzo in A minor, Op. 118, No. 1

Intermezzo in A, Op. 118, No. 2

Intermezzo in E flat minor, Op. 118, No. 6

Intermezzo in E flat, Op. 117, No. 1

Intermezzo in B minor, Op. 119, No. 1

Intermezzo in E minor, Op. 119, No. 2

Intermezzo in C, Op. 119, No. 3

Rhapsodie in E flat, Op. 119, No. 4

Walzer, Op. 39, for Piano-duet

Sonatas for Violin and Piano:
  1. G, Op. 78
  2. A, Op. 100
  3. D minor, Op. 108

Sonatas for Viola and Piano:
  1. F minor, Op. 120, No. 1
  2. E flat, Op. 120, No. 2

Sonatas for Clarinet and Piano:
  1. F minor, Op. 120, No. 1
  2. E flat, Op. 120, No. 2

Piano Trios:
  1. B, Op. 8
  2. E flat, Op. 40 (Horn)
  3. C, Op. 87
  4. C minor, Op. 101

Piano Quartets:
  1. G minor, Op. 23
  2. A, Op. 26
  3. C minor, Op. 60

Piano Quintet in F minor, Op. 34

F. Chopin

Fantaisie in F minor, Op. 49

Scherzo in C sharp minor, Op. 39

Ballade in G minor, Op. 23

Nocturne in D flat, Op. 27, No. 2

Nocturne in C minor, Op. 48, No. 1

Valse in E flat, Op. 18

Etude in A flat, Op. posth.

Etude in D flat, Op. posth.

Mazurka in D, Op. 33, No. 3

Mazurka in F sharp minor, Op. 59, No. 3

C. Debussy

Préludes, Ier livre:
  7. Ce qu'a vu le Vent d'Ouest
  8. La Fille aux Cheveux de Lin
  10. La Cathédrale engloutie

Préludes, 2me livre:
  6. General Lavine, Eccentric

Soirée dans Grenade (Estampes)

Poissons d'or (Images, 2me série)

A. Dvořák

Three Romantic Pieces for Violin and Piano, Op. 75

Piano Quintet, Op. 81

G. Farnaby

A Toye

H. Ferguson

Sonata in F minor

Five Bagatelles

C. Franck

Prelude, Fugue and Variation (arr. Bauer)

Sonata in A for Violin and Piano

Piano Quintet

G. F. Handel

Sonatas for Flute and Piano:
  3. G
  5. F

J. Haydn

Sonata No. 37 in D

Piano Trio No. 7 in A

Works played by Myra Hess at the National Gallery

T. Matthay
Albumblatt
Elves

W. A. Mozart
Sonata in G, K.283
Sonata in A, K.331
Sonata in F, K.497, for Piano-duet
Sonata in D, K.448 for two pianos
Sonatas for Violin and Piano:
   E minor, K.304
   F, K.376
   B flat, K.454
Piano Quartet in G minor, K.478
Piano Concertos:
  1. D, K.175
  2. B flat, K.238
  3. C, K. 246
  4. E flat, K.271
  5. F, K.413
  6. A, K.414
  7. C, K.415
  8. E flat, K.449
  9. B flat, K.450
 10. D, K.451
 11. G, K.453
 12. B flat, K.456
 13. F, K.459
 14. D minor, K.466
 15. C, K.467
 16. E flat, K.482
 17. A, K.488
 18. C minor, K.491
 19. C, K.503
 20. D, K.537
 21. B flat, K.595

M. Peerson
The Fall of the Leaf

H. Purcell
Saraband in G minor, Z.661/4
Minuet in G, Z.660/3
Air in G minor, Z.T693/2

S. Rachmaninoff
Prelude in B minor, Op. 32, No. 10

D. Scarlatti
Sonata in D, L.14
Sonata in B minor, L.33
Sonata in G, L.387

F. Schubert
Sonatas:
  3. A, Op. 120
  7. A minor, Op. 164
 10. B flat, Op. posth.
Impromptu in B flat, Op. 142, No. 3
Dances
Piano Trio in B flat, Op. 99

R. Schumann
Papillons, Op. 2
Carnaval, Op. 9
In der Nacht, Op. 12, No. 5
Etudes Symphoniques, Op. 13
Bunte Blätter, Op. 99
Andante and Variations, Op. 46, for two Pianos, two Cellos and Horn
Piano Quintet in E flat, Op. 44

A. van Wyk
Poerpasledam, for Piano-duet

(Groups of songs by Beethoven, Brahms, Schubert and Schumann for Elena Gerhardt; of Debussy songs for Maggie Teyte; and of Bach, Dowland, Monteverdi and Schubert for Roland Hayes.)

Discography

BY

F. F. CLOUGH & G. J. CUMING

PART I: COMMERCIAL RECORDINGS

A: 78 R.P.M. ISSUES

English Columbia Numbers	U.S.A. Columbia Numbers	Titles	Approx- Year of Issue
—	9062M o.n. 7151M	Debussy: La fille aux cheveux de lin Poissons d'or & Minstrels	c. 1928
—	9074M o.n. 50199D	Brahms: Capriccio, b mi. Op. 76/2 Mendelssohn: Songs without words Op. 38/6 & Op. 67/4	do.
—	9072M	Falla: Ritual Fire Dance Griffes: The White Peacock	do.
—	4082M o.n. 157M	Ravel: Pavane pour une infante défunte (2 sides)	do.
—	4083M o.n. 168M	Scarlatti: Sonatas, C, L.104; c mi., L.352 Beethoven: Bagatelle, B flat, Op. 119/11 Brahms: Intermezzo, C, Op. 119/3	do.
D 1635	4084M o.n. 2063D/M	Bach-Hess: Jesu, Joy of Man's Desiring Bach: French Suite No. 5 – Gigue	do.

112

English Columbia Numbers	U.S.A. Columbia Numbers	Titles	Approx-Year of Issue
—	4085M o.n. 1931D	Bach: Toccata, G, BWV 916 Allegro only Prelude & Fugue, c sharp mi., BWV 848	do.
—	4086M o.n. 252D	Palmgren: Cradle Song, Op. 17/9 Schumann: Vogel als Prophet, Op 82/7	do.
9509–12 (o.n. L 2103–6)	set M 91	Schubert: Trio, B flat, D.898 (*with Y.d'Aranyi & F. Salmond*)	1928
L 2119–21	set M 87	Schubert: Sonata, A, D.664 (5 sides) Rosamunde — Ballet music, G	1928
DB 1232	in set M 234	J. Field: Nocturne No.4, A Chopin: Nocturne, F sharp mi, Op. 15/2	1931
DB 1235	do.	Macdowell: Sea Pieces, Op. 55/3 Dvořák: Slavonic Dance, Op. 46/1 (*with Sir H. Harty*)	1931

(these two discs from Columbia History of Music, vol. IV)

English Columbia Numbers	U.S.A. Columbia Numbers	Titles	Approx-Year of Issue
LX 497–500	set M 266	Brahms: Trio, C, Op. 87 (*with Y.d'Aranyi & G. Cassadó*)	1936
LX 641–3 (auto: LX 8336–8)	set M 312	Beethoven: Cello Sonata, A, Op.69 (5 sides) (*with E. Feuermann*) – side 6 not Hess	1937

English H.M.V. Numbers	U.S.A. Victor Numbers		Approx-Year of Issue
B 8758	—	Matthay: Album Leaf, from Op.22 Elves, Op. 17	1938
B 9035	4538	Bach-Hess: Jesu, Joy of Man's Desiring Scarlatti: Sonata, G, L.387	1940
B 9189	—	Brahms: Capriccio, e mi., Op. 76/2 Intermezzo, A flat, Op.76/3	1941

(these last four sides re-issued at 45 r.p.m., 7EG 8281)

English H.M.V. Numbers	U.S.A. Victor Numbers		Approx-Year of Issue
C 2942–5 (auto: C 7486–9)	set M 473	Schumann: Concerto, a mi., (8 sides) (*with orchestra cond. W. Goehr*)	1937
C 3008–10 (auto: C 7508–10)	set M 476	Schumann: Carnaval, Op. 9	1938
C 3226	—	Brahms: Intermezzo, Op. 117/1 Intermezzo, Op. 119/3 Capriccio, Op. 116/7	1941
C 3237–8	—	C. Franck: Variations Symphoniques (*with City of Birmingham Orchestra, cond. B. Cameron*)	1941
C 3335–7 (auto: C 7580–2)	—	H. Ferguson: Sonata, f mi. (5 sides) Purcell: Sarabande; Menuet; Air	1943
C 3423	—	H. Ferguson: Five Bagatelles	1945
C 3960	—	Bach-Hess: Adagio, C (from Organ Toccata) Bach: Little Prelude No. 4, D	1950

B: LONGPLAYING 33⅓ R.P.M. ISSUES

English Numbers C – Columbia P – Philips	*U.S.A. Columbia Numbers (H – Harmony label)*		*Approx-Year of Issue*
C.33CX 1091 P.ABL 3219	ML 4568	Mozart: Concerto, E flat, K.271 (*with Perpignan Festival Orchestra, cond. P. Casals*)	1952
P.ABL 3184	ML 4701 (& in set SL 182)	Schumann: Piano Quintet, E flat, Op.44 (*with I. Stern, A. Schneider, M. Thomas & P. Tortelier*) – reverse side not Hess.	1953
P.ABR 4063	ML 4702 (& in set SL 182)	Brahms: Piano Quartet, c mi., Op. 60 (*with J. Szigeti, M. Katims & P. Tortelier*)	1953
P.S 06624R (Europe – 2 sides)	ML 4707 (& in set SL 183)	Schubert: Violin Sonata (Duo), A, D.574 (*with J. Szigeti*) – reverse not Hess	1953
P.ABL 3113	ML 4709 (& in set SL 184)	Brahms: Piano Trio, B, Op. 8 (*with I. Stern & P. Casals*)	1953
P.A 01207L (Europe)	ML 4710 (& in set SL 184)	Brahms: Piano Trio, C, Op. 87 (*with J. Szigeti & P. Casals*)	1953

(This series recorded at the 1952 Prades Festival)

re-issues from 78 r.p.m.	ML 4678	Beethoven: Cello Sonata, A, Op. 69 (*with E. Feuermann*) – reverse not Hess	1953 LP
	H 7119	Schubert: Sonata, A, D.664 Piano Trio, B flat, D.898 (*latter with Y.d'Aranyi & F. Salmond*)	

English H.M.V. Numbers	U.S.A. Numbers V – Victor A – Angel		Approx-Year of Issue
XLP 30005 o.n. ALP 1169 (tape: HTA 22)	V. LHMV 1068 A. 35705	Beethoven: Sonata, E, Op. 109 Sonata, A flat, Op. 110	1954
BLP 1039	V. LHMV 1062	Schumann: Concerto, a mi., Op. 54 (*with Philharmonia Orchestra, cond. R. Schwarz*)	1954
BLP 1061	A. 35591	Schumann: Etudes Symphoniques, Op. 13	1954

(BLP 1039 & 1061 now re-issued, coupled, on HQM 1014)

| BLP 1103 | A. 35591 (omits items †) | Scarlatti: Sonata, c mi., L. 352 Sonata, G, L. 387 Beethoven: †Für Elise (*a*) †Bagatelle, E flat, Op. 126/3 Mendelssohn: Song without Words No. 47 Granados: La Maja y el Ruiseñor Brahms: Waltz, A flat, Op. 39/15 Intermezzo, C, Op. 119/3 Bach-Hess: Jesu, Joy of Man's Desiring (*a*) | 1959 |

(items marked (*a*) re-issued at 45 r.p.m. on 7P 271)

PART II: NON-COMMERCIAL RECORDINGS, ETC.

(The following exist or have existed, but were not available on public sale. Copies of certain of the extant recordings are held by the British Institute of Recorded Sound, 29 Exhibition Road, London, S.W.7.)

E.M.I. UNPUBLISHED RECORDINGS: MATRICES DESTROYED

Recorded 1942:   Mozart: Concerto, C, K.467 (*with Hallé Orchestra, cond. L. Heward*)

Recorded 1945:   Haydn: Sonata No. 37, D

Discography

B.B.C. RECORDINGS

Discs

4845–51 30cm, 78 r.p.m. 7 discs	Brahms: Piano Quintet, f mi., Op. 34 (*with Griller String Quartet*): from National Gallery Concert, 25 August 1942
14363–5 30cm, 78 r.p.m. 3 discs	TALK by M. Hess: 'Teachers of Music – Tobias Matthay': recorded 7 Dec. 1949, broadcast 15 Dec. 1949
MX 15331 1 side	Bach-Ferguson: Lute Suite, c mi., BWV 997 – Sarabande Bach: Toccata, G, BWV 916
MX 15331–2 3 sides 40cm, 33⅓ r.p.m.	Schumann: Carnaval, Op. 9: Recorded 13 October 1950
27560, 27878 30cm, 78 r.p.m.	EXTRACTS from an Interview with John Amis: Recorded 7 June 1962

Tapes

T 27804	Bach: Prelude, G, BWV 902; English Suite, a mi., BWV 807: Broadcast 2 Nov. 1956
T 27890	Haydn: Sonata No. 52, E flat: Broadcast 3 Jan. 1962
T 28024	Beethoven: Concerto No. 4, G, Op. 58 (*with B.B.C. Empire Orchestra, cond. E. Fogg*) Broadcast 31 May 1938, B.B.C. Empire Service (copied from discs)
—	OBITUARY TALK on Tobias Matthay, 30 Jan. 1958

B.B.C. TRANSCRIPTION SERVICE DISCS

(The numbers are side numbers: all are 30 cm, 33⅓ r.p.m.)

104450–2	with Isaac Stern, violin H. Ferguson: Sonata No. 2 Brahms: Sonata No.2, A, Op. 100 Schubert: Sonatina No.1, D, D.384 Beethoven: Sonata No. 10, G, Op. 96

Recorded from Edinburgh Festival, Usher Hall recital, 28 Aug. 1960

95137–9	with B.B.C. Symphony Orchestra, cond. Sir Malcom Sargent Beethoven: Concerto No.5, E flat, Op. 73

Recorded from B.B.C. Promenade Concert, Royal Albert Hall, 12 Sept. 1957

CROWN FILM UNIT RECORDINGS

Mozart: Concerto, G, K 453 (*with R.A.F. Symphony Orchestra, cond. Wing-Com. R. O'Donnell*)

Beethoven: Sonata Appassionata, f mi., Op. 57, 1st movement only

EXTANT TAPES OF AMERICAN RADIO BROADCASTS
(SO FAR AS KNOWN)

Beethoven: Concerto No. 3, c mi., Op. 37 (*with N.B.C. Symphony Orchestra, cond. Toscanini*) — 24 Nov. 1946

Beethoven: Concerto No. 4, G, Op. 58 (*with Boston Symphony Orchestra, cond. Koussevitsky*), incomplete — ? 1946

Brahms: Concerto No. 2, B flat, Op. 83 (orchestral details not to hand) — ? 1956

Mozart: Concerto, A, K.414 (*with American Chamber Orchestra, cond. Scholz*) — March 1956

Mozart: Concerto, E flat, K.449 (*with New York Philharmonic-Symphony Orchestra, cond. Stokowski*) — Nov. 1947

Mozart: Concerto, d mi., K.466 (*with New York Philharmonic-Symphony Orchestra, cond. B. Walter*) — March 1956

Mozart: Concerto, C, K.467 (*with New York Philharmonic-Symphony Orchestra, cond. Stokowski*) — Feb. 1949

Mozart: Concerto, B flat, K595 (*with American Chamber Orchestra, cond. Scholz*) — March 1956

Schumann: Concerto, a mi., Op. 54 (*with New York Philharmonic-Symphony Orchestra, cond. Mitropoulos*) — Feb. 1952

PRIVATE TAPES

A public recital at the University of Illinois, Urbana, Ill., U.S.A: — March 1949

Bach: Partita No. 4, D, BWV 828
Schubert: Sonata, B flat, D.960
        Dances, Op. 9/36 (D.365)
                Op. 18/2, 9, 10, 12 (D. 145)
                Op. 33/1–7, 10, 14, 15 (D.783)
                Op. 50/1, 2, 13, 27 (D.779)
                Op. 77/3, 8, 9 (D.969)
                Op. 171/3 (D.790)

Discography

Brahms: Intermezzo, C, Op. 119/3
Scarlatti: Sonata, G, L.387
   (the last three items with remarks by M. Hess)

A public concert at the University of Illinois: March
                           1949

Mozart: Concerto, E flat, K.271
   Concerto, C, K.467
   (with the University of Illinois Orchestra, cond. ?)

(The compilers are indebted to Messrs. P. Saul, E. A. Hughes, Philip
L. Miller, H. Ferguson, and the Executors of the late Dame Myra Hess,
  for information and assistance for this compilation).